PENGUIN CANADA

THE WEST

Gerald Friesen grew up in Saskatchewan and was educated in Prince Albert, at the University of Saskatchewan and at the University of Toronto. He has taught at the University of Manitoba since 1970 and spent a year as the Seagram Chair of the McGill Institute for the Study of Canada in 1996-1997. He is a winner of the Canadian Historical Association's Sir John A. Macdonald Prize for his book *The Canadian Prairies: A History* and the American Association of State and Local History Award for *Guide to the Study of Local History in Manitoba*. He is also the author of *River Road: Essays on Manitoba and Prairie History*.

Understanding Canada

THE MCGILL INSTITUTE FOR the Study of Canada opened in Montreal in July 1994. Frankly, McGill is a wonderful place to study Canada. The university attracts thousands of students from across the country and internationally. Almost any class gathers French- and English-speaking students from half a dozen provinces and three or four countries. McGill faculty research and comment on Canada, from its bedrock to its latest cultural fads. Their networks involve colleagues from around the world.

The Institute—MISC to its friends—was founded by the Bronfman family as a new way to make Canada, its problems and its achievements, better known. Like other academic institutes, we organize courses, sponsor research, support younger faculty and graduate students. Our public education program promotes discussion of Canadian issues. Some of our winter conferences have been broadcast across Canada. Thanks to funding from the Seagram Company, MISC brought scholars from the Canadian West and the Atlantic provinces to help students and colleagues at McGill and other Quebec universities understand regional perspectives in Canada.

If MISC has a priority, it is helping Canadians understand issues. This is tougher than it sounds. Plenty of people think democracy works best with short sound-bites, dumbed-down slogans and a telegenic smile. Yet the information revolution drowns us in the complexity of problems. Solutions, however attractive, have side-effects. In health care, patients want to understand their condition so that they can give "informed consent." Why not citizens?

As humane people in one of the world's richest countries, Canadians wonder why poverty persists. Since we or our ancestors have come from somewhere else, are there better or worse ways to manage immigration? Canadians have a host of reasons, from trade to ancestral roots, to want the world to be a peaceful, prosperous place. What are our options to help make this happen? Or, as taxpayers, neighbours and, especially, as proud parents, we want to understand how schools work, who they sometimes fail, and how even good schools try to become better. The answers aren't easy, but they aren't rocket science either. The Understanding Canada series was conceived by MISC as a knowledgeable, sensible, sometimes wholly unexpected journey into issues that matter to Canadians.

If sharing understanding is MISC's goal, partnership with Penguin Canada comes naturally. Generations ago, an Englishman named Carleton Lane launched a series of blue and white paperbacks dedicated to making knowledge, from the classics to astral physics, available to everyone. Styles in reading and presentation have changed, but the ideals haven't. Understanding Canada is a series designed to connect people who know with people who want to understand. Let us know if it works—and where we go next.

Desmond Morton
McGill Institute for the Study of Canada
L'Institut d'études canadiennes de McGill
3463 Peel Street, Montreal, QC H3A 1W7

THE WEST

REGIONAL AMBITIONS, NATIONAL DEBATES, GLOBAL AGE

Gerald Friesen

PENGUIN
CANADA

A Penguin/McGill Institute Book

PENGUIN CANADA

Published by the Penguin Group

Penguin Books, a division of Pearson Canada, 10 Alcorn Avenue, Toronto, Ontario,
   Canada M4V 3B2

Penguin Books Ltd, 80 Strand, London WC2R 0RL, England

Penguin Putnam Inc., 375 Hudson Street, New York, New York 10014, U.S.A.

Penguin Books Australia Ltd, 250 Camberwell Road, Camberwell, Victoria 3124,
   Australia

Penguin Books India (P) Ltd, 11, Community Centre, Panchsheel Park,
   New Delhi – 110 017, India

Penguin Books (NZ) Ltd, cnr Rosedale and Airborne Roads, Albany, Auckland 1310,
   New Zealand

Penguin Books (South Africa) (Pty) Ltd, 24 Sturdee Avenue, Rosebank 2196, South Africa

Penguin Books Ltd, Registered Offices: 80 Strand, London WC2R 0RL, England

First published 1999

10 9 8 7 6 5 4 3 2

Copyright © 1999 by Gerald Friesen

Printed and bound in Canada on acid-free paper ∞

CANADIAN CATALOGUING IN PUBLICATION DATA

Friesen, Gerald, 1943–
The West: regional debate, national ambitions, global age

(Understanding Canada)
"A Penguin/McGill Institute book."
ISBN 0-14-028421-4

1. Canada, Western. 2. Regionalism — Canada, Western.
3. Canada, Western — Politics and government.
I. Title. II. Series: Understanding Canada (Toronto, Ont.)
FC3209.A4F74 1999   971.2'03   C99-930217-5
F1060.92.F7125 1999

Visit Penguin Books' website at **www.penguin.ca**

Table of Contents

To Max, Ben and Fiona,
Megan and the McGuires,
Brian, Katherine, Bob and Shelagh

THE WEST

REGIONAL AMBITIONS, NATIONAL DEBATES, GLOBAL AGE

Acknowledgments

THE WEST IS A NATIONAL ISSUE? If you had asked me at any point in the first half of the 1990s, I would have said no. Then in 1996–97, having spent a few months in central Canada, I discovered that some Quebecers and Ontarians, and even some Atlantic Canadians, had grave doubts about westerners' commitment to the country. It was as if the views being expressed by the West's makers of public policy and elected representatives no longer struck a chord with other Canadians. Or as if the issues and choices being debated in the West did not reflect Canadian values.

My uneasiness might have been forgotten had it not been reinforced by Des Morton, director of the McGill Institute for the Study of Canada, who suggested to me that the country was drifting apart and that the western half was no longer understood in the eastern half. His view was reinforced by a group of commentators at a national conference in 1998 who were asked to address the issue of "Accommodating the New West." Gordon Gibson, journalist and former politician, Tom Flanagan, political scientist at the University of Calgary, and Doug Owram, historian at the University of Alberta, asserted that the East seemed unwilling to accommodate the West, that the gulf between the two was larger than most people appreciated and that conversation across the divide had become difficult, if not impossible. I set to work in earnest.

My greatest debt in the preparation of this book is to Des Morton, who shepherded me through my term at McGill and who provided both encouragement and helpful criticism as the writing proceeded. To Gael Eakin, the staff and faculty at the institute, and the students, all of whom made my visit so pleasant, I say thank you. I would also like to thank Brian Young and Béatrice Kowaliczko, Suzanne Morton, and the History Department at McGill for so many kindnesses. In British Columbia, Keith and Molly Ralston, Bill and Peggy New, Wilson and Wilma Parasiuk, Ian and Elizabeth MacPherson, Grace and the Stewart family, Stewart and Hazel Andreen, and Bob Friesen and Shelagh Rae; in Alberta, the McGuire family, Ken Norrie, Ted Chambers, Robert Mansell, Herbert Emery and Maurice Doll, and the history curatorial staff at the Alberta Provincial Museum, as well as Michael Payne and Frits Pannekoek; in Saskatchewan, Tom and Signe Ferris, Jim Roberts, Brian and Lynda Allbright, Graham and Gordon Boyd, Jack and Chris Andreen and family, Don and Amy, Woody and Stephanie, and my mother and her friends in Prince Albert; in Manitoba, my colleagues and friends: you have helped me in many ways and I thank you very much. Parts of the argument were prepared for a Canadian studies conference on "Defining the Prairies" at St. John's College, University of Manitoba, and I am indebted to Robert Wardhaugh, Kathryn Young, Dennis Cooley and colleagues for convening a spirited debate. The University of Manitoba also provided me with a public forum to test some ideas, and again, I learned a great deal from the discussion and appreciated the support of Joanne Keselman, Gary Glavin and colleagues.

Jackie Kaiser and Penguin Books have been model taskmasters and I have enjoyed our work together. And a thank you to Maryan Gibson, who edited this book with care and dispatch.

To Jean and Joe, who were present for and contributors to this entire process, I say a heartfelt thank you.

Gerald Friesen
St. Paul's College
University of Manitoba
December 1998

Introduction

AN IMPORTANT EUROPEAN SURVEY of the globe written in the 1890s suggested that the northern section of North America, defined politically as the Dominion of Canada, "constitutes no distinct geographical unit." The theme was picked up a century later by the British Columbia geographer Cole Harris and expanded into a wonderful essay on the nature of Canada. Harris employed the vantage point of a nighttime transcontinental flight to suggest that the country "dissolves into an oceanic darkness spotted by occasional islands of light." And therein lay the metaphor of his essay: "Canada is a composition of islands," he wrote, an archipelago situated "between an implacable north and the United States."

Harris's essay reflects a common view. Because the geography of settlement is disjointed and discontinuous, Canadians are accustomed to thinking about their country in broad regional generalizations, regions being the names they apply "to blocks of country where they do not live," as Harris commented. Over the decades and centuries, inevitably, such broad terms as the West, Central Canada, the East, the North, labels that have "only fuzzy locational meaning," crystallized into something more. Indeed, they became "part of our vocabulary of spatial ambition and resentment."

The regional labels convey interpretations of broad community identities. At least, said Harris, at one time they conveyed reliable notions about the rhythms and realities of some Canadian community experiences over others. Thus, "in the older settlements of the Maritimes, the rhythms of the land, the traditional ways that earned a living, and the people who lived nearby comprised the context of most experience. Even today, genealogical conversation is a Maritime staple, a reflection of communities whose people have known each other through the generations."

By contrast, the West is not so rooted in history and in the chronicles of identifiable families. Harris writes: "In the West such conversation is rarer, for the local texture has been different, having less of custom and the generations and more of movement, technology, markets, and memories of other places."[1]

I want you to think about this statement in the pages that follow. Certainly there is truth in Harris's suggestion that Atlantic and Western Canadian societies differ in this way. But I want to argue that the West is, indeed, shaped by history, and that our perceptions of the past may stand in the way of our seeing its present reality clearly.

Think about the ten-gallon hats at the Stampede or Grey Cup parades, the eagle feather at a First Nations ceremony and the jellied salads at a Saskatchewan church supper. Are these not time-honoured items? They call up memories of an open frontier, of Native Canadian power and of the gospel-inspired co-operative movement. What could be more western than that?

And yet, do they not seem dated? This ambiguity interests me too. Like the hats, the feather and the salads, historical images of western regions are with us today. Despite their power, they convey assumptions that might have been outgrown years ago.

The West has taken a new shape in recent decades. In Part I of the book, I suggest that the old two-region vision of western Canada—the Prairies and the Coast—has been superseded by a single economic and social experience. Now we have one West, extending from the Lake of the Woods to Vancouver Island.[2]

In Part II, I suggest that this single West should also be seen in terms of a new trans-Canada reality, the centrality of the province in our public life. Each of the four provincial societies that comprise the West also possesses a distinctive political life and distinctive approaches to economic activity. Each has different, historically rooted party systems within which community choices are debated and made. In other words, though each province responds to similar global pressures and circumstances, it does so within its own, long-standing party loyalties and partisan assumptions.

In Part III, I return to the notion of a single West and consider the state of the regional political conversation. I propose that, despite the varying fortunes of political parties and the understandable preoccupation of the national media with the Reform Party (the winner of a majority of western Canada's seats in the federal elections of 1993 and 1997), the region is engaged in a quite conventional political debate between "right" and "left" choices in an age of globalization. In short, I reject Reform Party assertions about a western anti-government cultural bias.[3] I deny its broad generalization that the West's opposition to deficits and support for the traditional family dominates the Canadian political agenda. Instead, I argue that the West is riven by the same left–right debates in politics that one finds in any modern community. These debates concern the family and civil relations, the relative role of markets and the public sector, aboriginal policy, immigration levels and affirmative action programs, but also, as is inevitable in Canada, the nature of federal government institutions such as the Senate and the responses to be made to Quebec sovereignists.

The purpose of *The West* is to get Canadians to re-imagine one of the vast regions in the Canadian archipelago. By picturing these islands clearly—not at night out of an airplane window but in the light cast by the forces of a global age—we can visualize and debate the purpose and the choices of the nation. And we may find that cowboy hats, eagle feathers and jellied salads have as much to say in today's society as in a previous age.

REFERENCES

1. Cole Harris, "The Emotional Structure of Canadian Regional-ism" lecture delivered at McGill University, printed in *The Walter L. Gordon Lecture Series 1980–81*, volume 5, *The Challenges of Canada's Regional Diversity* (Toronto 1981).

2. Thus, the theme of such books as J.F. Conway's *The West: The History of a Region in Confederation* (Toronto: James Lorimer 1983), while very useful at one time, seems less helpful today.

3. Peter O'Neil, "Reform MP rejects traditional stereotype" in *Vancouver Sun*, 18 July 1998, B4. This is discussed further in chapter 8 "Alberta."

Part I

From Two Wests to One: History, Economy and Society

CHAPTER ONE

The Prairies and the Coast

THE OPENING SENTENCE OF W. O. Mitchell's first novel is one of the best-known statements of place in Canadian literature: "Here was the least common denominator of nature, the skeleton requirements simply, of land and sky—Saskatchewan prairie."[1] The Canadian Prairie provinces may be more varied than this suggests, but just as the scene on the old dollar bill could represent only one Canadian region, so do Mitchell's words.

Ethel Wilson's novels and stories capture British Columbia as effectively as Mitchell presents an enduring image of the Prairies. Wilson wrote of British Columbia—the lower mainland, the islands, the Interior, the north—with conviction and precision. She once said: "I have a lifelong love for this province of ours which I share with many people, this British Columbia, as if it were a person, as it is—and a person of infinite variety and inference." She wrote in a letter to Mazo de la Roche: "But *region*—that's a different matter. I'm all against conscious nationality in a novel (for a novel is about people and is universal), and *for* regionalism, *if* region means a lot to the writer."[2]

As characters slowly take form in Wilson's novels and stories, the province, too, unfolds:

> The Hope-Princeton Highway, like the Cariboo
> Highway, moves into British Columbia's heart. It
> leads to a mining country, and orchard countries,
> past lakes, rivers and mountains into the Boundary
> Country, fabulous with mines, with old ghost

towns, with thriving communities divided by
mountains and forests and waterfalling rivers, and
to and beyond the mighty and mysterious concentration at Trail. This was the road that Maggie
chose, at least as far as the river with the dancing
name Similkameen. . . . [3]

Mitchell and Wilson expressed a particular cultural moment, the
middle quarters of the twentieth century, when the country
embraced five or six great regions, and when landscape images
evoked keen reactions among generations familiar with—if slightly
removed from—work and life on the land. In that world, there were
two Wests, one the Prairies, and the other just B.C., or the Coast.

Today, by contrast, there are four Wests, because each western
province is increasingly definable, and there is one West, an overarching regional presence in national conversations. The four
provinces differ in their political character, in the mix of sectors
within their economies and in the face they present to the world. Yet
they share broader responses to the contemporary age. This transition—from two to four regions and from two Wests to one—is fundamental to understanding this part of Canada.

I

WHEN THE BRITISH NORTH American colonies—Canada (East and
West), Nova Scotia and New Brunswick—drafted their Confederation documents between 1864 and 1867, annexation of the vast
northwestern reaches of the continent was a crucial part of the plan.
Despite the resistance at Red River in 1869, when Louis Riel
imposed new conditions on the transfer, Manitoba and the North-
West Territories entered Confederation in 1870. British Columbia
also exacted stiffer terms than John A. Macdonald had expected, but
its accession made the transcontinental project complete in 1871.

Canada's first three decades appear rocky in retrospect, and
national survival was far from assured. The country saw numerous
conflicts: an armed Métis uprising in the North-West in 1885 that
prompted the dispatch of 5,000 troops; a Nova Scotia legislature resolution favouring secession; continuous battles over the
place of the French language and Roman Catholic religion that
set citizen against citizen in New Brunswick, Quebec, Ontario and
Manitoba; a close-run financial adventure in completing the
Canadian Pacific Railway (the rail connection was part of the deal

promised B.C. upon its entry into Canada); and contests between federal and provincial governments that led to the convening in 1887 of the first premiers' conference and a political attack on the government in Ottawa. All these and more bore witness to the depth of national uncertainty and the intensity of struggles to define a new society.

Improvement in the international economy in the late 1890s, along with some good fortune in the timing of Canada's entry into Europe's emigration sweepstakes, fuelled boom times for the next decade. Not even the Great War snuffed out all this prosperity. In parts of the country, including the West, expansion—in cycles of prosperity and recession—continued to the end of the 1920s. Then, however, the Great Depression brought the good times to a halt.

The years from 1867 to 1940 saw the creation of the Prairies, a distinctive region built on wheat. The society was everywhere mixed in race and religion. Because each district seemed to offer a different combination of nationalities, the Prairies could be described as uniform in their diversity. And because Ottawa retained control of all Manitoba and North-West public land, as well as natural resources (the Prairies being alone among the regions of Confederation to live with such a restriction), this West was surveyed, homesteaded, administered and policed according to principles that Ottawa applied regionwide. This was the Canadian West of the boom era, exaggerated by immigration propaganda and popular expectation, and said to be poised to lead Canada and even the British Empire.

The Prairie metropolis was Winnipeg. As W.L. Morton, the historian of these Prairie times, wrote, Winnipeg was "never a merely provincial city."[4] From its offices and warehouses and marshalling yards were dispatched the railway cars, the catalogue goods and the administrative regulations that served two generations of farms and villages.

Winnipeg housed the Grain Exchange and the speculators, the *Grain Growers' Guide* and the co-operators, the social gospel professors and the chautauqua stars, the political operatives and their corporate allies—in clubs, banks and railway offices—for whom this entire region seemed an empire in the making and for the taking. As late as the Second World War, Winnipeg's population was greater than that of all the other Prairie cities combined; its cultural life was diverse, and its journalistic debates on women's suffrage, pacifism and unions were intense and searching.

Despite the superficial uniformity of survey and purpose, there was great variation in a territory that stretched a thousand miles by seven hundred miles on the schoolchild's map. Indeed, the northern half—drawn on the diagonal from Winnipeg to the Peace River country in northwestern Alberta—was nearly untouched except by the fur trade and local lumber operations. The far southwest was cattle country. In the east, hundreds of miles of Shield rock and forest separated the region from the settled areas of Ontario and Quebec. And in the agricultural areas, patterns of moisture, frost and soil type distinguished zones of better and lesser fortunes from those of absolute loss. Whatever the leading ethnic group in a local district, the towns were mainly British Canadian. Some observers thought Manitoba was more Ontarian, Saskatchewan more British, Alberta more American. Nonetheless, the cultural tone of the region was a distinctly Prairie version of English-speaking Canada, one expressed in the imperial views of the history texts, in the Protestant "non-denominational" notes of the schoolroom's daily Bible reading and in the parliamentary rules governing every official public meeting, from the municipal council to the wheat-pool board, the Women's Missionary Society and the grade four Red Cross assembly.

The Canadian Prairies constituted a region. From the 1870s to the 1930s, the territory and the non-aboriginal community could be perceived as one entity. Oil and politics and communications technology changed this community identity during the generation after the Second World War, as the individual provinces, and an inclusive West, grew in prominence.

II

BRITISH COLUMBIA WAS NEVER a part of the Prairie West. It was always another place, the west beyond the West, the Coast.

On the occasion of its centenary celebration—measured from 1858 to 1958, a suitably non-Canadian point of reference for a separate people—its historian, Margaret Ormsby, described the B.C. community as "a people who make their home on a transmontane slope which had always been a world in itself." But Ormsby went on to insist that B.C. residents were both Canadian and British:

> And yet, this world has never been completely
> isolated from other communities. For the first colo-
> nists on Vancouver Island, the sea had provided the

bond with England; for the fur-traders, and later
for the settlers, the Fraser River had provided an
arterial highway to Canada. British Columbians
had been formed into strong individualists by their
rugged mountain setting, and they had been set
apart by distance, but because of the sea and the
great river, they had their bonds with the world
outside.[5]

This image that B.C. is different has been expressed many
times. The Scots fur trader, Duncan Finlayson, who served as one of
the leaders of the Hudson's Bay Company, first travelled to the
Pacific as a junior officer in 1831. He wrote in his journal how
surprised he was to discover that the Rockies constituted an extraordinary divide:

The effect which so total a change of climate &
scenery produces is really astonishing. The eye can
fix on no one object which is not directly the
reverse of any thing to which it has been accustomed even on the east side of the mountains. The
trees, Birds, insects & flowers all wear a foreign
aspect—by its over-flowing abundance all nature
here demands attention. In the summer the air is
usually dry, clear & with little rain & the heat is
much moderated by refreshing breezes from the
Ocean—In winter the atmosphere is much cooled
by the frequent rain & the months of Decr and
Jany still more so by frost.[6]

A century later, Bruce Hutchison, the journalist, made the same
observation: "Crossing the Rockies, you are in a new country, as if
you had crossed a national frontier. Everyone feels it, even the
stranger, feels the change of outlook, tempo, and attitude. . . . We
cannot go back to our old homes east of the mountains. In our
hearts we never recross that barrier."[7]

What is different about British Columbia?

Winter, for a start. Compare the rain forests of the Coast to the
stark, frozen landscapes of the Prairies on a typical January day. And
then add the diversity of environment that accompanies the Gulf
Islands, the valleys of the Interior, the Peace River plain and the
northwestern forest.

Then there are the racial mixtures. Contrast the Asian presence in early British Columbia with the range of Europeans then living on the Prairies. And consider the density and wealth of the coastal aboriginal peoples in the context of plains and parklands hunting households.

The economy differs, too. The industry of the Prairies is grain; in B.C. it's the fisheries, forestry and mining. In the province's towns, mines and camps, British Columbians thought of themselves as belonging to the working class, whereas a prairie farm family could not be fitted easily within any class.

British Columbia also had its own metropolis. By the beginning of the twentieth century, only Vancouver could challenge Winnipeg for leadership of the West, and in time, it surpassed Winnipeg. Vancouver was part of the lower mainland and, like Winnipeg, its regional population accounted for more than half the provincial total. It controlled the financial and economic life of the province. It was Canada's Pacific port and western rail terminus, as well as the hub of provincial transportation networks. After the opening of the Panama Canal in 1914, Vancouver extended its hinterland into the Prairies at the expense of Winnipeg; by the end of the 1920s, about forty percent of Canada's grain exports travelled west to its harbour rather than east through the Manitoba capital towards Thunder Bay and the Great Lakes to the Atlantic. Inevitably Vancouver became a focus for education and the arts, as well as business.

At British Columbia's heart lay the elite—the class of business, government, military and church leaders who, as in the rest of the British Empire, shaped society's norms and distributed its rewards. Margaret Ormsby suggested that this elite was created in the 1890s, an era she labelled "The Great Potlatch":

> The wealth of the governing group, derived chiefly from investment in land, transportation systems, mines, lumbering, salmon canneries and flour-mills, had been accumulated quite suddenly, and as everyone was frank in admitting, only because the railway and the steamboat had provided access to additional markets. . . . The Smithe government had established a precedent in using public lands, a seemingly inexhaustible asset, to bonus the construction of wagon roads and railways and to pay the costs of reclamation

schemes. The succeeding administrations dis-
pensed subsidies of land, mineral and timber
rights with bold and munificent gestures.[8]

Historians debate whether B.C. society was divided more by
race or by class. They do not disagree that the divisions, in both
cases, placed citizens in opposing camps. Their disagreement, simply, is over the cause of the sharpest conflicts in the community.
Ormsby, writing in the 1950s about turn-of-the-century politics,
said, "In no other part of Canada were working-men as radical as in
British Columbia."[9] In discussing the Asiatic Exclusion League of
1907 and its parade that degenerated into a mob invasion of Asian
districts of Vancouver, she noted, too, the threat of "an ugly and
growing racial tension." Outbreaks of labour and racial violence on
"the Island" (Vancouver Island) in 1913 were incendiary, Ormsby
acknowledged, and anti-Sikh sentiments associated with the landing
of the Komagata Maru in 1914 demonstrated that such incidents
had many origins.[10]

The race issue also attached labour to the middle class. Robert
McDonald's history of Vancouver demonstrates that class and race
worked together in the years before 1914 to distinguish the
respectable from the rough, and the citizen from the outsider. The
outsiders were born in Europe or Asia, or were Native Canadian,
and lived in shacks along the harbour edge or, later, after these
dwellings were torn down, in a distinct inner core of the city. They
were often single, their jobs temporary, and they participated hardly
at all in the civic institutions that governed their existence.[11]

The Prairie tradition of attacking Ottawa did not find a parallel
in British Columbia. Forestry and mining, both under provincial
jurisdiction, offered little basis for federal-provincial conflict.
Fishing, a hot spot in Ottawa-Victoria relations today, did not raise
such disputes in B.C.'s early years because Ottawa's supervision was
relatively benign. Thus, no habit of discontent of the Prairie type
developed, no oppositional reflex, that would unite B.C.'s population
against the "outsider" or, in this case, the national government.[12]
Indeed, local leaders expressed disdain for the lawyers and loggers of
Ottawa, a mere timber town on the Rideau.

British Columbia was, in short, a distinctive second West in
Canada. Jean Friesen has written:

> It can be argued that this distinctiveness is a myth,
> a variation in a pervasive North American culture,

discernible only to the eye of faith. But, even so,
the myth has grown and expanded and has contributed to a conviction among both citizens and
outside observers that British Columbia is, as
Charles Mair suggested so long ago, *sui generis*, "in,
but not of Canada."[13]

III

A single West and four provincial Wests superseded the two-region
model in the generation after the Second World War. As the following chapters suggest, the pattern was clear by the 1970s and by
the 1990s unmistakable. The individual provinces became the
organizing forces in much of Canadian life after 1945. Next to
nation and locality, a citizen's province was the most prominent
expression of his or her public identity. Moreover, in the multilevel
system of government in Canada, the province became the crucial
agent in teaching residents to become citizens. The consequence
was an intensified provincial identity in every part of the country.

The division of tasks between levels of government has proved
surprisingly flexible in Canada. Ottawa's assumption of sweeping
responsibilities during wartime illustrated what could happen in an
emergency. But so, too, the increases in provincial authority after
1945 demonstrated that the powers could be transferred both ways.
Canadians now live with regular federal-provincial conferences,
serious debates about such matters as federal-provincial contracts on
social policy, and noteworthy transfers of administrative responsibility from Ottawa to the provincial governments, such as those in
the fields of immigration and training. As a result, Ottawa has
declined in relative power and the provinces have gained greater
prominence in citizens' daily lives.

The transition from two western regions, the Prairies and the
Coast, to four western provinces has had an impact on western
Canadian history. The provincial governments have grown rapidly
in jurisdiction and public importance. The institutions they super-
vise have become items of greater daily importance and so are subject to more urgent debate. This talk finds its focus in provincial
party systems and in provincial capitals.[14]

The shifts in governmental structure have been accompanied by the development of provincial communications networks.

Newspapers, radio and television created provincial, not regional, public conversations. Thus, for example, school radio (and later television) broadcasts originated in the provincial capitals and were disseminated as part of provincial curricula and reinforced the schoolchild's identification with the province. I sang "Saskatchewan, Saskatchewan" heartily in grade six in the mid-1950s, and doubtless most other graduates of Prairie schools in that generation can cite at least one similar hymn. We all recognize the existence of provincial licence plates, flowers, flags, birds, tartans and so on, which the province employs to establish its place in our minds.

An opportunity and stimulus for the establishment of a provincial alternative to the national "imagined community" occurred on the occasion of major anniversaries: Saskatchewan and Alberta in 1955 (fiftieth) and 1980 (seventy-fifth), British Columbia in 1958 (a centenary), and Manitoba in 1970 (also a centenary), all organized significant programs of celebration in which citizens paid tribute to its "pioneers." The theme of these events was that this particular province could lay claim to being a distinctive, and slightly superior, society. Superior to whom? Anyone you might care to mention, but chiefly those other Canadians next door and, of course, our neighbours to the south.

The reasons for the emergence of a single West are more elusive. Indeed, many residents of the Prairies and B.C. vigorously dispute that any such entity exists. They contemplate the natural charms of their distinctive environments—the northern lights, the mountain slopes, the particular tang of the air, the quality of snow—and insist that a prairie, parkland, foothill, or valley is paramount in their sense of place. And for many people, this is true. But, while these responses to a distinctive environment are undeniably powerful, there is more to be said.

The old two-region notion built on wheat and lumber seems less convincing today than the parallel concepts of four provincial economies and a single, overarching western economy based on primary product exports, growing urban manufacturing and expanding cultural and services sectors. The fabled frontier of Stetsons and cow ponies has to share top billing with dense urban zones in which the inhabitants are more familiar with Mountain Equipment Co-op and snowboards. Next to that image of string ties, jellied salads and square dances one must find room for Sarah McLachlan, kd lang and Tina Keeper. And these new sectors are prominent across the four western provinces.

Similarly, the national political conversation, which once distinguished the Prairies from British Columbia (often forgetting B.C. in the process), now utilizes generalizations about the West with great regularity. With the legitimacy provided by the "first past the post" electoral system, members of Parliament claim to be speaking for the entire region from Lake of the Woods to Vancouver Island whenever it is plausible to do so.

If one thinks in terms of economy and society, therefore, rather than environment or specific staple exports, one can perceive a fundamental change in Canadian regional perceptions during the twentieth century: from two Wests (the Prairies and the Coast) in the years before 1945, to four Wests (each a province) and to a single, overarching West during the second half of the twentieth century.

REFERENCES

1. W.O. Mitchell, *Who Has Seen the Wind?*

2. Ethel Wilson, "The Bridge or the Stokehold: Views of the Novelist's Art" in *Canadian Literature* 5 (Summer 1960) 44, and Wilson to de la Roche, 20 August 1955, cited in David Stouck, ed. *Ethel Wilson: Stories, Essays and Letters* (Vancouver: UBC Press, 1988), both quotations cited in Jean Barman, *The West beyond the West: A History of British Columbia* (Toronto: University of Toronto Press 1991) pp. 353, 317.

3. Ethel Wilson, *Swamp Angel* (Toronto: Macmillan 1954) pp. 34–5.

4. W.L. Morton, *Manitoba: A History* (Toronto: University of Toronto Press 1957, 1967) p. viii.

5. Margaret A. Ormsby, *British Columbia: A History* (Toronto: Macmillan 1958, 1971) p. 494.

6. Duncan Finlayson, "Trip across to the Columbia 1831." Hudson's Bay Company Archives, Winnipeg E/12/2, pp. 18–20.

7. Bruce Hutchison, *The Unknown Country: Canada and Her People* (Toronto: Longmans, Green 1942) p. 315, cited in Barman *The West beyond the West*, p. 353.

8. Ormsby, *British Columbia*, pp. 305, 307.

9. Ormsby, *British Columbia*, p. 331.

10. Ormsby, *British Columbia* 349–54, 365–71.

11. Peter Ward and Robert McDonald, *British Columbia Historical Readings* and Robert A. J. McDonald, *Making Vancouver: Class, Status, and Social Boundaries, 1863–1913* (Vancouver: UBC Press 1996).

12. Donald E. Blake, "Western Alienation: A British Columbia Perspective" in A. W. Rasporich, ed. *The Making of the Modern West: Western Canada Since 1945.* (Calgary: University of Calgary Press 1984) pp. 55–62.

13. Jean Friesen, "Introduction" in Friesen and H.K. Ralston, eds., *Historical Essays on British Columbia* (Toronto: McClelland and Stewart, 1976) p. vii.

14. It is noteworthy that the very vehicle for carrying and diffusing West–East protest in Confederation shifted from the federal party system to the system of federal-provincial negotiations during the century. Again, the flexibility of the Canadian system of government is striking.

   There were some uniquely prairie aspects to the rise of provincial societies. Ottawa gave up much of its special responsibility for the prairie West in 1930. Thereafter, control over public lands and natural resources resided with the provincial governments. The North-West Mounted Police became the Royal Canadian Mounted Police in 1919. Certain powers remained in Ottawa, notably over international trade, wheat exports and aboriginal affairs, but the contrast between the first and second national policies, not to mention the vast shift when the third national policy began in the 1980s, was sufficient to offer convincing reasons for the decline of federal control of prairie communities.

CHAPTER TWO

The Export Economies

FROM THE 1870s TO the 1940s, there seemed to be one dominant economic pattern in western Canada: the various communities scattered across this vast land belonged to "a small, open, resource-rich, export economy." This phrase, devised by economist Kenneth Norrie, constitutes a deceptively simple generalization.[1] It conceals the fact that, before the 1940s, despite broad similarities, two very different community economic experiences evolved, that of the Prairies and that of British Columbia. The Pacific province's economy grew steadily and rested comfortably above the national average in income and employment. The Prairie provinces' economy fluctuated wildly, travelling through heady booms and then descending into truly wrenching periods of recession. Then, after 1945, despite variations from province to province, the dramatic swings were replaced by a steady convergence in growth, employment and income.

I

Fur, fish, forest, field and mine sustained western fortunes for most of the century after Confederation. The products travelled mainly to markets outside the country—in Europe at the turn of the twentieth century and, increasingly, in the United States after 1950. But decade in and decade out, B.C. producers fared better in international markets than their Prairie counterparts.

Prairie producers were at the mercy of the rain and the sun. And inevitably, global weather patterns affected not just the yields

of crops around the world, but also the price received by producers when they sold their goods on a grain exchange. Furthermore
the Canadian influence in these markets was small in relation to the
production that could now be conveyed to any buyer from any part
of the globe. Thus, the exigencies faced by Canadian farmers
meant nothing to a buyer of wheat in Liverpool who could turn to
American, Australian, Indian or Argentinian crops to make up a
shortfall. Fluctuation of income became the story of the Canadian
Prairies.

Resource depletion and environmental destruction may seem
to be today's, not yesterday's, concern. But such crises have a long
history and they, too, underlie prairie income fluctuations. The
Prairies' export economy began with the fur trade in the
eighteenth and nineteenth centuries. By the 1870s, this trade was
valued at perhaps a million dollars a year by the Hudson's Bay
Company alone. It continued to earn substantial returns for the
next half-century and then began to fluctuate wildly, as it still
does.[2] Within the usual cycles in the populations of fur-bearing
animals, these districts endured several episodes of environmental
destruction that stand out in the history of North America. During
the nineteenth century, the buffalo, once estimated to be fifty
million in number, were reduced to a few hundred. Though it is
often seen as unique, this slaughter parallels other environmental
losses, notably the sharp decline of sturgeon in western Canadian
Shield lakes.

The next great export from the West, wheat, similarly brought
environmental change to the Prairies. In the decade after 1905, the
Canadian government pushed back the ranching frontier in southwestern Saskatchewan and southern Alberta and encouraged the
homesteading of this vast arid tract of short-grass prairie. Most of
the settlers, including the family of novelist Wallace Stegner, who
wrote *Wolf Willow*, a wonderful memoir about his childhood in this
territory, found that the land was simply too dry and the varia-
bility of rains too great for them to establish viable grain farms.[3]
Thousands moved out, starting in the dry years of 1917-21 and continuing through the 1920s.

Then came the darkest decade in prairie history—the dirty
thirties. It is reported that the sun disappeared behind clouds of
blowing soil and that, in one storm in the spring of 1934, a single
cloud of dust stretched from Alberta to Texas, suffocating birds
in the sky and dusting ships some miles off the Atlantic coast.

Millions of tons of top soil vanished and thousands of farm animals died or had to be slaughtered. This decade marked the low point in prairie incomes in the twentieth century and the greatest example of income fluctuation—that between 1928 and 1932—in this century.

II

BRITISH COLUMBIANS SAILED ABOVE the national income averages throughout the first three-quarters of the twentieth century. Indeed, in the late 1920s and through the difficult decade of the 1930s, the personal income per capita of the province was about one-third higher than the Canadian average and marginally higher than in the next-richest province, Ontario. This margin shrank slightly between the 1940s and the early 1970s, but British Columbia still attained a personal income per capita of ten to twenty percent more than the national average during this entire span.

Such statistical measures are somewhat misleading, of course. By dividing income equally across the entire provincial population, they ignore the inevitable fact that some families received a great deal more than the average while many others received much less. Nonetheless, the per capita income tables do measure the total amount of income available for distribution in the province and, to that degree, offer a gauge of relative provincial wealth.

British Columbia was built on four pillars in the early years— agriculture, mining, fishing and forestry. As the decades passed, fishing declined in relative importance and forestry grew increasingly productive. By 1980 the largest primary industries in the province were forestry ($3.9 billion), mining ($2.7 billion) and agriculture ($.8 billion). Add to this the manufacturing that was part of forestry (approximately half the value of all manufacturing shipments, or $8.6 billion), and forestry can be said to have accounted for sixty percent of the provincial exports, more than one-eighth (13.3 percent) of the provincial GDP, and ten percent of the labour force.[4]

Deviation from Trend of per Capita Total Income, Wages and Salaries, and Farm Income in the West Compared with those in Ontario, Canada 1926–45 and 1945–81

| | AVERAGE DEVIATION FROM TREND (in percent) | | | | | |
| | TOTAL INCOME | | WAGES AND SALARIES | | FARM INCOME | |
	1926–45	1945–81	1926–45	1945–81	1926–45	1945–81
Ontario	13.1	4.8	12.1	4.1	28.5	18.9
Western Canada	22.3	8.6	13.1	5.2	72.9	27.8
Prairie provinces	26.7	9.8	13.1	4.9	82.7	30.2
Manitoba	17.3	7.2	12.5	4.4	59.5	33.4
Saskatchewan	38.6	14.4	13.4	6.5	95.6	38.4
Alberta	25.4	9.0	13.3	5.3	57.6	25.5
British Columbia	12.4	6.8	11.3	6.2	22.1	12.2

Source: Based on data from Statistics Canada
Economic Council of Canada, *Western Transition* (Ottawa, 1984) p.13 .

British Columbia lived on its natural resources—forests, minerals, fish and fields—for most of its first century in Confederation. Like the Prairie provinces, it exported most of these goods, either to the rest of Canada or, increasingly, to the United States and the world. However, it did not sustain as devastating reverses as did the Prairies in the drought in the 1930s.

British Columbia did not inspire a myth like that linking Prairie campaigns for economic security to a "second national policy." As Margaret Ormsby, the historian of the province during the post-1945 generation, wrote, B.C. grew into a "class-divided society...."[5] In the rest of Canada, she said, "the strange course of British Columbia politics earned for the province the reputation of a maverick."[6] Its economic diversity and prosperity left the image of a favoured, though factional, province. The picture contrasted sharply with the Prairie farm experience. B.C. seemed to be a community in which considerably greater income, along with milder climates, made possible a more ample existence.

I I I

THE PRAIRIE PROVINCES EXPERIENCED a dramatic drop in personal income per capita during the late 1920s and remained at very low levels, just above those for the Atlantic region, until 1941. This income per capita then rose towards the national average in the mid-1940s and remained near or just below that point for the next thirty years.[7] In retrospect, it appears that the post-1945 generation in western Canada benefitted both from the institutions of the new welfare state and from the introduction of new economic activity.

The year-to-year variation in per capita income before 1945 was far greater in the three Prairie provinces, especially among those who relied on farm income, than in Ontario or British Columbia.[8] Prairie people, notably dwellers in rural Saskatchewan and Alberta, bore the brunt of this exceptional volatility in material fortunes.

Atlantic Canadians might well reply that their region was poorer, and remained poorer, throughout this century. This is true, but nevertheless, it is only human nature that Prairie dwellers were moved to oppose the unfairness of sharp fluctuations in their own income. They had had good times, they had lost them, and they wanted to regain that favoured state.

The reduced degree of income fluctuation in the Prairies after the Second World War demonstrates that the regional economies underwent significant changes between 1945 and 1975. Why the difference? One reason, provided by the Economic Council of Canada, was an increase in the number of service-sector jobs, most of which paid steady, decent salaries.

A second reason, so obvious it requires little elaboration, was the extraordinary resource boom in the West that began with the Leduc, Alberta, oil strike in 1947 and continued through the 1950s as a result of additional resource investments and steady export sales. These enterprises touched every provincial economy. They included minerals, oil and potash in Saskatchewan, mine and hydro developments in Manitoba.

A third reason concerns the farm economy itself and, in particular, the role of science in smoothing out the great fluctuations of earlier days. Prairie Canadians did learn from the disaster of the 1930s. The Prairie Farm Rehabilitation Administration taught families how to take advantage of retention ponds, shelter belts, trash farming (in which weeds are left on the land) and new cultivation equipment. Herbicides, insecticides and fertilizers became a

part of farm science and contributed to higher crop yields.[9] A fourth
reason, one that causes a great deal of angry debate in the contemporary West, concerns the role of the state in income stabilization.
Prairie Canadians, or so the heartwarming story goes, wisely used
the government—the state—to make ends meet. The little guy was
victorious over entrenched big interests; the struggle was framed as
W.R. Motherwell versus the Winnipeg grain barons (1901–1914),
A.J. MacPhail versus the international grain markets (1921–1930),
or Tommy Douglas versus the American Medical Association
(1944–1962). Whatever the incarnation, the theme once set prairie
hearts aflutter.[10]

An opposing interpretation has taken shape in the 1980s and
1990s. In this view, the Prairie economic miracle is described as a
victory achieved *in spite of* government and *in spite of* some Prairie
leaders' foolish attachment to idealistic social-gospel nonsense. But
more of this in a moment.

The drama opens with ordinary farm families doing everything
in their power to improve their odds of survival. Thus, for example,
they won a deal on freight rates, the Crow's Nest Pass agreement,
signed in 1897 and renewed after the First World War, which was
widely regarded as the western equivalent of the central Canadian
manufacturer's tariff protection: it ensured that an artificially low
rate would apply to Prairie grain as it headed to market, whether via
eastern or, in later years, western ports.

This was just the first of many political victories. Farm families
campaigned for and won federal government supervision of the institutions of the grain trade, including inspection of the grading, weigh-
ing and mixing processes at every stage of the grain's journey to
market. On their own initiative, they created co-operative elevators
to handle and market the grain, co-operative stores to supply farm
and household alike with consumer goods, and co-operative financial
institutions (credit unions, or *caisses*) to meet their credit and banking
needs. But still the farms were plagued by income fluctuation.

Their largest single victory was the longest in coming. They
might grow two blades of wheat where only one had grown before,
they might reduce the cost of farm and household, and they might
ensure fairer treatment by railway companies in the movement of
goods to market, but could they influence the international market
itself? Creditable government grain sales during the unstable years
around the close of the First World War convinced farm families
that this was the answer: a single government selling agency for farm

crops. It took fifteen years, and the rise and fall of a voluntary alternative—the wheat pools—but in 1935, just before his government lost the general election, R.B. Bennett passed an act creating the Canadian Wheat Board. During the Second World War, when markets were again unstable, the Mackenzie King government made this agency the single monopoly seller of Canadian wheat abroad. The Wheat Board has occupied this role ever since and has from time to time assumed additional responsibilities for other crops. The board has been a fundamental source of income stability for Prairie grain farms for the past fifty years.

How should Canadians view this remarkable record of successful interventions by Prairie families to make their farms just a little less vulnerable to economic forces? Today opinion is divided.

At one time, as noted above, the typical Prairie storyteller might have described the local experience as democracy in action and justice secured. In this perspective, the Wheat Board, the cooperatives, the Canada Grain Act, the Crow's Nest Pass freight-rate agreement and all the other institutions won by farm households, from Dominion Experimental Farms to Better Farming Trains and university extension services, ensured that ordinary people might have a fair deal. Such measures would offset the accidents, acts of God and plain bad luck that otherwise could destroy a household overnight.

If the region had been built according to the dictates of Sir John A. Macdonald's National Policy, it was made a better place by Prairie reformers. So successful were they, in their own minds, that they claimed credit for the emergence of a second national policy. The Wheat Board might be seen as part of this loose system, and so might such institutions as the Canadian Broadcasting Corporation. After all, the national radio system permitted farmers and working people from coast to coast to talk together, to study together and thus to address the social and economic ills that confronted them.[11]

Government interventions in society during succeeding decades can also be located within this undeniably social democratic interpretation of Canadian history. Unemployment insurance, the family allowance, institutionalized collective bargaining, hospital and medical insurance, and improved old age pensions could all be categorized as part of the second national policy. All represented state intrusions into the marketplace, and each provided a means of shielding ordinary families from the excesses of competitive capitalism.

Prairie Canadians should not try to take all the credit for this long list of national legislation that instituted Canada's welfare state. Nor should social democrats claim a unique and solitary role in the process. After all, most of it was initiated by Liberal governments between 1935 and the early 1970s, and some of the rest came about as a result of actions taken by the Bennett and Diefenbaker Conservative administrations.

Yet Prairie dwellers did have a right to claim that they belonged in the vanguard of these campaigns. It was Premier Bracken of Manitoba and John Dafoe, editor of the *Winnipeg Free Press*, who pressed for a system of national equalization grants that would tax the richer provinces to ensure a minimum standard of social and educational services in the poorer ones. It was the CCF government in Saskatchewan that first introduced hospital and medical insurance. But for the rest, westerners were simply part of countrywide movements and, indeed, part of international trends in government.[12]

How would today's antisocialist forces view such an interpretation of western history and Canada's welfare state? First, they would depict the outcome not as justice achieved but as freedom lost. Regina journalist Don Baron explains:

> It can be seen now that those crusading social gospellers, with their all-out assault on capitalism and the free market, were oblivious to one vital truth—competition and the free market are the very basis of wealth production and personal freedom. In a calamitous oversight, they held righteously to their ideology.[13]

Baron ties the early heroes of farm protest, W.R. Motherwell and T.A. Crerar, to a program that sought merely to make the market work better. Until the early 1920s, in other words, western Canada was developing nicely. But then the utopians, adherents of a Christian social gospel message, tried to legislate more than was possible in a government managed by mere mortals. Thus, Baron sees the Wheat Board, the social gospel of the churches and CCF political doctrines as deviations from the proper path of capitalist discipline. Big governments and clumsy state institutions prevented the market from working its magic through the allocation of rewards and penalties. Farmers had let grain marketing "get bogged down in politics" and had neglected the "hard-nosed business of getting [grain] to market."[14]

The two approaches, one favouring the welfare state and the other competitive individualism, are equally ideological. Both are shaped by responses to the market and to the international capitalist system in which market principles are embedded. To western reformers, such as the farm families who struggled to establish co-operatives, medical insurance and the Wheat Board, the worst features of markets could be controlled by government intervention. Conservatives, in contrast, believed that prosperity could best be secured by the operation of market forces. Whichever side one favours today, it can still be agreed that Prairie income fluctuations after 1945 were much smaller than they had been before the Second World War. And government intervention, as an important aspect of the expansion of the service sector, must have played a role in the change.

There were two economic stories in western Canada in the seventy-five years after Confederation. The Prairie provinces lived through several environmental disasters and endured exceptional volatility in income. B.C. residents, though similarly reliant on natural resource wealth, enjoyed stable and much higher incomes on the average than their Prairie compatriots. The trend, though, which became noticeable in the 1960s and 1970s, was to smaller fluctuations and greater regional equality in per capita income.

REFERENCES

1. Kenneth H. Norrie, "A Regional Economic Overview of the West Since 1945" in A. W. Rasporich, ed. *The Making of the Modern West: Western Canada Since 1945* (Calgary: University of Calgary Press 1984) pp. 63–78.

2. Arthur J. Ray, *The Fur Trade in the Industrial Age* (Toronto: University of Toronto Press 1990).

3. Wallace Stegner, *Wolf Willow: A History, A Story, and a Memory of the Last Plains Frontier* (New York: Viking Press 1966).

4. Economic Council of Canada, *Western Transition* (Ottawa: Supply and Services Canada 1984) p. 41.

5. Margaret Ormsby, *British Columbia: A History* (Toronto: Macmillan 1958, 1971) p. 486.

6. Ormsby, *British Columbia* p. 491.

7. Economic Council of Canada, *Living Together: A Study of Regional Disparities* (Ottawa: Supply and Services Canada 1977) pp. 34–43.

8. Economic Council of Canada, *Western Transition* (Ottawa: Supply and Services Canada 1984) pp. 11–14.

9. It is noteworthy that the lessons were not imprinted on every mind. In recent decades, trees have been removed from many prairie fields, sloughs have been ploughed, and erosion is once again an issue. Moreover, the invasion of weeds, not a problem before the twentieth century, has raised a new environmental challenge: herbicides have become a part of most farmers' economic planning, but what will such materials do to the soil? And to the very weeds themselves? Clint Evans's doctoral dissertation, University of British Columbia, addresses the history of weeds in western Canada.

10. The first two episodes are discussed in V.C. Fowke *The National Policy and the Wheat Economy* (Toronto: University of Toronto Press 1957), and the third in Robin Badgley and Samuel Wolfe

Doctors' Strike: Medical Care and Conflict in Saskatchewan (Toronto: Macmillan 1967).

11. This interpretation comes from a leading Prairie economic historian, V.C. Fowke, in "The National Policy—Old and New" in *Canadian Journal of Economics and Political Science* 1952. It is elaborated in Janine Brodie *The Political Economy of Canadian Regionalism* (Toronto: Harcourt Brace Jovanovich 1990).

12. Donald Sassoon, *One Hundred Years of Socialism: The West European Left in the Twentieth Century* (London: I. B. Taurus 1996).

13. Don Baron, *Canada's Great Grain Robbery* (Regina: the author 1998) p. 16.

14. Baron *Canada's Great Grain Robbery* p. 93.

CHAPTER THREE

Resource Industries
and Rural Economies Today

WHAT IMAGE IS EVOKED by the words "western Canada"? If Canadians were asked to respond, would they produce a list that includes
vast green forests? flat wheat fields and sentinel grain elevators?
snowcapped mountains and beautiful foothills? flat stretches of land
dotted with oil derricks?

These are time-honoured depictions of the West. The images
betray a cultural lag, however, because they are so clearly drawn
from the natural world. All of them are associated with rural sites
and resource-based activities—forests, farms, energy exports and
tourism in natural surroundings. Their variety suggests the fabulous
resource wealth of western Canada and its special natural attrac-
tions. For people who live in the West, though, such a list seems
slightly old-fashioned—a reminder of another age. Indeed, the
alterations in western circumstances during the present generation
are so profound that Canadians living outside the region might be
surprised by the scale of the changes. These recent changes have a
common Western character.

I

THOUGH NATURAL RESOURCES STILL provide the foundation of the
western economies, the changes in these industries since the 1960s
and especially since 1988 will be a revelation to those unfamiliar
with the contemporary scene. The new developments are evident in
every one of the western provinces and in all the major primary
products: petroleum and natural gas, wood and paper, grains and

animal production, and the water-linked resources that range from fish and hydro power to water itself.

The West was once a society built on hundreds of rural communities. Now it is constructed on a few metropolitan districts, about a dozen in total. In addition, it contains several dozen small cities and the surviving few hundreds of towns and villages, reduced from the few thousands of the 1920s. It also relies on a relatively small population in farm districts and resource communities, many of the latter in northern sections of their provinces, far removed from concentrations of people and power.

The rural and resource activities have been responsible for a remarkable volume of goods destined for international consumption. And therein lies a profound contradiction: this is a rural world in precipitous decline, leaving aging residents in emptied villages where once had been youthful hopes and a viable society. It is also a vigorous, competitive, globally oriented economy producing more goods at lower costs than ever in history. Though many rural communities may seem to be sad places, simply struggling to hold on in the face of overwhelming change, some individuals in the resource industries have never been so busy or so rich.

The catalogue of rural change, East and West, is extensive. The number of Canadian farms in eastern Canada, as well as in the West, dropped by hundreds of thousands after the Second World War. In the East, the area devoted to field and animal husbandry decreased by millions of acres. In the West, significantly, though the number of farms dropped, there has not been a comparable loss of land under cultivation. Employment in fishing, whether on the Pacific or Atlantic coasts or in the inland lakes, has plummeted. Forestry operations in eastern Canada now employ far fewer workers. In the West, however, where vast new territories have been opened and new species of trees harvested, the number of jobs has held firm. In both East and West, entire networks of rural communities, including sports, churches and schools, as well as economic services, have ceased to be viable.

What is causing this revolution in rural life? Technological innovation. Exceptional advances in resource production equipment (ships, tractors, tree-harvesting machines, computer-assisted animal husbandry and oil exploration technologies) have made workers' labour infinitely more productive. The combination of trucks and inland grain terminals and giant fish plants and oil pipelines offers flexible, cheaper means of handling these goods. Moreover, the

Internet, television, school buses and big-box shopping centres at
the edges of cities provide accessible, efficient means of meeting
entertainment, educational and consumption needs.

In retrospect, observers have distinguished three national economic policies. The first, developed by Sir John A. Macdonald in
the 1870s and 1880s lasted until the interwar years. The second,
largely a product of federal Liberal governments, endured until the
1970s. The third has been acquiring a clearer definition in recent
decades.

During the half-century after 1945, the extensive investments in
farms and villages across the rural margins of the country were simply abandoned—wasted—because that society was itself increasingly
uneconomic. And on the Prairies, where a vast network of villages
relied on horse, elevator and railway transport, the rate of abandonment was breathtaking. The first national policy had simply encouraged investors to build too intensively, given the scale of farming
and forestry and energy production work that became possible after
1945. Moreover, the social programs of the second national policy,
which sustained individual incomes and basic community services,
actually slowed the adjustment to changing market realities by making life in these districts more attractive than it might otherwise
have been. However, according to Michael Troughton,

> while stabilization [the second national policy]
> did provide greater security of income to the
> minority of farmers able to adopt the increasingly
> industrial model of agriculture, it did nothing for
> the marginal producers beyond hastening their
> demise, while at the same time contributing to the
> need of the majority of remaining farmers to secure
> off-farm employment to maintain family income.[1]

These drastic revisions have actually increased in pace during
the past twenty years. It has become apparent, in fact, that a *third*
national policy began to take form in the 1970s and 1980s. Its clearest statement was the 1985 report of the Macdonald Royal Commission on the economy, which recommended that Canada abandon
the nation as the basic organizing unit for most aspects of production and marketing. Instead, the commissioners suggested, Canada
should adopt free trade with the United States. In the next ten years,
the American free trade deal was signed (it went into effect on January 1, 1989), a larger pact integrated Mexico into this free trade

zone (the North American Free Trade Agreement began in 1993), and now, under the Chrétien government, Canada has embraced even more fully the market and worldwide competition. The abandonment of the old rural order seems complete.[2]

The foundation of the original grain export system in the Prairies was provided by the Crow's Nest Pass freight rate agreement. It imposed artificially low rates on the shipment of Prairie grain to export terminals. By the 1970s, under pressure from railway companies and advocates of greater reliance on market forces, the federal government opened a series of investigations into the policy. Defenders of the family farm and the agricultural village argued for the retention of the Crow; opponents said it prevented economic diversification and militated against investment in the rail and handling systems. Between 1980 and 1998 the entire rate system was dismantled and rebuilt. For many farmers, the cost of shipping grain actually tripled between 1994 and 1998. The original small homestead in the old grain export system could not survive. A related casualty was the prairie village.[3]

This story of rural decline is familiar in every region in Canada. It is also well-known in the United States and Australia. It is not so common in Europe. The contrast is worthy of note.

To some observers, those who favoured the traditional rural society, the new environment seemed sterile and the government economic policy heartless. These critics argued that Canada could have adopted an alternative approach to global economic strategy, as the European Union had done, by paying careful attention to the protection of rural communities. Such critics claimed that the federal government had moved rather more quickly than the European model permitted:

> The aim of EU rural and regional policies is not to preserve anachronistic systems artificially, but to avoid the problems of collapse of traditional economies and communities and the absolute loss this entails. Programs seek to make it possible for as many persons as possible to remain and for change to be gradual and linked to retaining a settled and functioning rural hinterland. Besides protecting communities and local economic and social capital, policies encourage development of labour intensive activities such as recreation and tourism.

> An underlying goal is the retention of continued
> and viable occupance of as much of the ecumene as
> possible, utilizing rural persons and resources *in
> situ*, and allowing rural residents to continue a
> rural way of life.[4]

To judge from their policy decisions, neither the Mulroney nor
the Chrétien governments found reason to follow such a rural strategy in Canada. From the perspective of a resource community or
farm household that lost its gamble with the market, the story of the
past five decades has been not just constant change but also failure
and loss. Vast stretches of the country appear, in this light, to be
irrelevant. Indeed, one recent proposal would give the Prairie grass-
lands to Aboriginal people and return the plains to buffalo pasture.[5]

The contemporary circumstance of the rural west, nevertheless,
is much more than doom and gloom. There are numerous individual
cases of success. The optimism has been driven in part by rural agricultural adaptation. In the five years between the 1991 and 1996 cen-
suses, the decline in Prairie farm population and farm numbers was
negligible. Two other trends stood out in the census: many farm
operators held an additional job off the farm; and the new capsule of
advice to farmers—go bigger, go niche—was reflected in the increase
in average farm size and in the range of specialty crops.[6] The rapid
growth in hog production and the investment in hog processing
plants demonstrates that the catchphrase represents actual investment and noteworthy, if risky, change.

The scale of the loss can also be discerned in the census figures.
As late as 1941, two Prairie residents lived in rural settings for every
one who lived in an urban neighbourhood. (Note that "urban" was
defined as a centre larger than 1,000 population, a fiction that actually underestimated the size of the rural community in relation to
the urban.) About half the Prairie workforce was gainfully employed
in agricultural occupations.

Today, Alberta and British Columbia are overwhelmingly
urban—eighty percent of residents dwell in cities and towns. Even
Saskatchewan and Manitoba are mainly urban.[7] Fewer than eight percent of the western population is engaged in agricultural occupations
and, if one adds all other workers in primary industries such as mining, oil wells, fur, fish and forestry, the total employed in the primary
sector is less than twelve percent, or one in eight workers.

From the perspective of those who have sustained substantial dislocation, the past few decades have constituted an era of loss in western Canada's rural and resource communities. Those who have adapted successfully see a brighter picture.

II

THE ALTERNATIVE DEPICTION OF western Canada's rural and resource history focuses on economic success, not failure; growth of a new infrastructure, not community collapse; increased production and larger volumes of exports, not declines in the income of unfortunate individuals; and diversification, not mono-crop labour and the dilemmas of the "staple trap."[8]

How can such a different impression emerge from the same set of facts? The answer lies in the export trade figures and in the production gains that lie behind them.

Take just two examples. In the 1960s and 1970s, Canadian farms produced about 17 million metric tonnes of wheat; in the 1980s and early 1990s, output had increased to about 28 million. Similarly, the canola crop in the 1970s averaged about two million metric tonnes; in the 1980s and early 1990s it averaged 3.5 million. These dramatic increases in agricultural productivity and in the capacity of the transportation system, gains of sixty-five percent and seventy-five percent respectively, were matched in other leading export sectors. Yet the workforce engaged in primary industries had dropped and so had the rural population. The productivity increases represented a kind of economic miracle.

Total merchandise exports from western Canada nearly doubled between 1988 and 1997.[9] Such an expansion of output was due mainly to shipments of primary products. Oil and gas exports represented about one-third of all western Canadian merchandise exports, forest products about one-quarter, farm products about one-eighth, and minerals, fertilizers and chemicals one-tenth.[10] Thus, these shipments alone accounted for nearly eighty percent of total exports.

In the early 1980s, the economist Kenneth Norrie could argue that a staple- or export-based theory of economic growth was largely sufficient to understand the political and economic history of post–1945 western Canada. His view would need to change only a little if he were asked to review the economic changes during the intervening years.[11]

Primary product exports remain at the heart of the western Canadian economy. To the degree that these goods travel outside

Canadian borders (and two-thirds of the goods, measured by value, do so), then the Western Canadian worker and owner are at the mercy of fluctuations in the relative value of currencies and of international supply and demand. In other words, the rural and resource economy continues to dominate western Canadian fortunes despite the dramatic changes of the past two decades. The area's economic fortune lies beyond the control of local actors in the sense that prices and markets are shaped by forces outside the local economy.

This volatility is not reduced by another significant difference in the new economy. The signing of the FTA and NAFTA in 1988 and 1993 respectively has emancipated the flow of staple goods, particularly petroleum and natural gas, from national policy influence. For better or worse, the export of these primary products is much more at the mercy of the market, and much less under the aegis of the national government, than it was before.

The change is noteworthy. Advocates of market-based approaches to the economy, including supporters of rapid increases in energy exports, welcome this continental integration. They prefer that markets, not governments, shape the export business. Those who are more cautious in their analysis of long-term energy supply and more fearful of environmental degradation regret it. They claim that Canada's increased reliance on market signals produces short-sighted thinking on precisely these matters.

The relative role of the market and the roller coaster of boom and bust in energy exports figure prominently in discussions of western Canadian public policy. British Columbia and Saskatchewan have significant energy industries, but Alberta is the overwhelming force in these discussions. When the price of oil was low, as it was in mid-1998, Albertans again became cautious, even nervous, as they contemplated a slowdown that might mean a return to the depressed eighties. But the Alberta preference for market, not national, decisions on price, export volumes and environmental regulations still outweighed any concerns about local recessions.

III

A THIRD THEME IN western Canadian resource development, alongside the rural decline and the resource boom, concerns the industries that are locked in debates over their very viability. Among these, forestry and fishing stand out. To make matters more complicated, aspects of these issues involve two levels of government.

The chief protagonists are British Columbia and Ottawa; the chief issues include responsibility for the environment and, perhaps more pressing, for international trade relations. The conflicts between the two levels of government over jurisdiction make complicated problems even worse, leaving the American intervenors to watch in amazement from the other side of bargaining tables.

Fishing is not as important as it once was to the British Columbia economy, accounting for about $400 million in landings in 1996, or less than .5 percent of provincial activity. Even within the fishery, groundfish and shellfish are now larger components of the catch than the original leader, salmon. But nothing is likely to heat up Ottawa–Victoria and U.S.–Canada debates more than a salmon war. For each year of the 1990s, indeed, the debates and protests have been intense.

The British Columbia government has taken the side of salmon conservation and asked whether the Americans can be trusted. Premier Glen Clark has declared, "Protection of Canada's salmon must be seen for what it is—not a regional issue but a matter touching on the national interest in conservation of our salmon," and described federal negotiating positions as "nearly treasonous." The Canadian government has tried to maintain diplomatic conversations via Washington with the states of Alaska and Washington while seeking a settlement on quotas and seasons. It, too, claims to be working in the interests of conservation.

The future of the commercial fishery is in doubt. Though you might wish to question its credentials in making such a blanket statement, a *Globe and Mail* editorial pronounced that there is "unlikely to be a viable commercial salmon fishery on the West Coast in 15 years' time." Given its economic and environmental vulnerability, the fishery question is, inevitably, a hot political issue.

The forestry industry is far more important to the British Columbia economy. It accounts for nearly fifteen percent of the provincial workforce directly or indirectly, for twenty percent of the province's gross domestic product and a slightly larger proportion of the provincial government's revenue (about twenty-two percent).[13] As energy dominates Alberta, so forestry dominates B.C.

The forestry debates centre on two matters, trade and conservation. The trade issue is affected by fortunes in the Asian economy, to which B.C. exports $2 billion in softwood lumber and more than $400 million in wood pulp annually.[14] It is also affected by the Free

Trade Agreement. For twenty years, Canadian softwood-lumber
shipments to American markets have irritated producers in the U.S.
This is due, in part, to the B.C. government's alleged generosity to
business in its royalty and conservation policies. The debate seems
endless. Indeed, a "final" 1996 deal intended to appease American
competitors threatened to unravel two years later under conditions
of depressed Pacific trade.

B.C. and Ottawa have to negotiate with each other as well as
with the Americans. Naturally relations are often frosty. Premier
Clark has declared that he would defend his province's "sovereign
right" to manage the forest; his declaration reminded observers of
Alberta Premier Peter Lougheed's frequent statements in the early
1980s on control over oil, or Saskatchewan's Allan Blakeney on
potash in the mid-1970s.[15] And once again, as in periodic battles
with the United States over energy and grain exports, western and
national interests did not necessarily coincide.[16]

The forest industry has fierce critics within B.C. itself. Though
Europeans have heard more about baby seals and luxury furs, the
political struggle among Canadians over the conservation of the
country's natural heritage has centred on the old-growth rain forests
more than any other single issue. During the 1990s, in succession,
Canadians were made aware of remote mountain valleys where
stands of ancient trees were being cut: South Moresby Island,
Meares Island, Carmanah Valley, Stein Valley, Clayoquot Sound,
King Island and Great Bear Rainforest—each became the rallying
cry for an environmental campaign. Greenpeace, which was born in
B.C., is the grandfather of these nature wars, but it has been joined
by many new experts in street theatre as the years have passed.[17]

The battle has also become more precise. The original goal of
the environmental campaign was the preservation of wilderness
areas. Now, nine million hectares (nine percent of the province) fall
under the rubric of protected parkland. An additional fifty million
hectares is said to remain in a wilderness state. For many activists,
the target became a particular forestry practice—clear-cutting—
which they claimed led to increased erosion and the destruction
of biodiversity, and thus constituted an environmentally destruc-
tive approach to harvesting trees. By lobbying in European markets, the environmentalists have moved some way towards securing
their goals. In 1998 the giant forestry company, MacMillan
Bloedel, announced that it would phase out clear-cut logging
within five years—a decision described by one commentator as

"the most profound change in forestry practices since the beginning of the century."[18] The battle may soon be moving on, this time to Alberta's aspen forests and the larger area of boreal forest, or taiga, of which they form a part.[19]

While the front pages featured the logging battles, newspapers' "job wanted" columns hinted that B.C. forests and fisheries were acquiring a different economic role. Tourism has become a valuable industry in western Canada, and nowhere more valuable than in the Pacific fjords and the forested and mountainous areas that comprise the B.C. and Alberta wilderness. Tourism revenues in B.C. were estimated at $6.3 billion in 1994. Though much of this money was spent in Vancouver and Victoria ("two of the top twenty tourist cities in the world," boasts the minister of tourism), it was lured to the province by the promise of wilderness, whether by cruises along the Pacific coast, skiing at Whistler and other mountain resorts, sport fishing, whale watching, trail riding, river rafting or any of the other pastimes of the "SuperNatural" province.[20]

A final natural product must be noted: that is, whether western Canada wants to get involved or not, there looms eventually a continental battle over Canadian water resources and, thus, over the prospect of water exports. In B.C., as one interested lawyer noted, much of the water resource is renewable: "It falls from the sky in annual deluges unparalleled elsewhere in the world except Alaska." The argument presented by this enthusiast concludes: "The trick for British Columbians to master is how to set a fair price for a resource that will allow the development of the industry and ensure that the benefit goes into the provincial treasury rather than into the pockets of foreign or multinational corporations."[21] There are several other intervening steps. Acts of the federal and provincial governments already prohibit interbasin transfers of river water and absolutely prohibit the export of water in large volumes. The B.C. Water Protection Act, for example, forbids the export of water in containers larger than twenty litres. Meanwhile, the southwestern United States, particularly parts of Arizona, Nevada and California, look northward with increasing urgency. The debate over western Canadian water has just begun.

IV

A SIGNIFICANT DIFFERENCE IN the pre– and post–1970 Wests concerns relations between local economies and the federal government's national economic policies. The signing of the two free trade agreements has resulted in a new economic circumstance, whether one is considering control over the volume of energy products heading south, over the transition now taking place in western agriculture, over salmon conservation or over environmental and trade considerations in the forestry industry. What does this mean for Confederation?

Consider, first, the direction of Western Canadian export trade. Where do the products of western Canada, the goods that are not consumed within the West itself, actually go? Over forty percent of the total exports travel south to the United States. About thirty-two percent go to the rest of Canada (twenty-three percent to Ontario, and nine percent to Quebec and the Atlantic provinces). Of the rest, about sixteen percent go to Asia, seven percent to Europe, and four percent to the rest of the world.[22]

This is a substantially different picture than prevailed in the first half of the twentieth century. Then, western Europe and Canada itself were the main markets, wheat and lumber were the products, and farming and forestry were the occupations. What is amazing is both how complete the change has been and how rapidly it has been effected. The regionalization of the North American economy must be recognized for what it is and its implications considered carefully.

The decline of federal economic power over the west and the change of direction in trade flows have altered the old balance of forces in Confederation. Both introduce new circumstances into the calculations of Canada's political leaders. The increasing reliance on market forces and the declining influence of federal government regulations probably reduce the stress on Ottawa–West relations. However, the decline in interregional trade and the increase in western Canadian–American trade, especially in energy and forest products, also reduces westerners' contact with and knowledge about the rest of Canada. Thus, the recent changes in the rural and resource economies of western Canada offer new challenges for the Canadian nation. They also speak of a single economic pattern between the Lake of the Woods and the Pacific. The fact that these recent changes are superimposed on older regional expectations and loyalties reinforces the popular assumption that there is only one West in today's Canada.

REFERENCES

1. Michael Troughton, "The Failure to Sustain Rural Canada" in *National History: A Canadian Journal of Enquiry and Opinion* 1:1 (1997) p. 5.

2. Janine Brodie, *The Political Economy of Canadian Regionalism* (Toronto: Harcourt, Brace, Jovanovich, 1990).

3. Barry Wilson, "Demise of Crow subsidy forces change" special report in *Western Producer* 9 April 1998.

4. Troughton, "The Failure to Sustain Rural Canada" pp. 56–7.

5. Don Gayton, "The grass and the buffalo" and other essays in his *The Wheatgrass Mechanism: Science and Imagination in the Western Canadian Landscape* (Saskatoon: Fifth House Publishers 1990); the buffalo proposal is discussed in A.H. Paul, "The Popper Proposals for the Great Plains: A View from the Canadian Prairies" in *Great Plains Research* 2/2 (1992).

6. Tsvetelina Parvanova, "Fewer farmers tilling the soil" *Winnipeg Free Press* 16 December 1997, B4.

7. The population ratio is sixty-three percent urban to thirty-seven percent rural in Saskatchewan, and seventy-two percent urban to twenty-eight percent rural in Manitoba.

8. Canadian economist Harold Innis suggested that in new settler societies such as Canada, entrepreneurial energies focused on the export of a few staples, leading to an unbalanced reliance on these commodities. Since the entire economy would be vulnerable to price swings for a few goods in external markets, it would be much more unstable than would one that relied on a variety of productive activities.

9. Merchandise exports increased from just under $40 billion in 1988 to about $77 billion in 1997.

10. Oil and gas exports—32.8 percent; forest products—23.4 percent (sawn lumber 14.3 percent; pulp and paper 9.1 percent); farm products—12 percent; mineral, fertilizer, chemical—

10 percent. Stephen Janzen and Edward J. Chambers, "The Alberta and Western Canada Export Experience under the Free Trade Agreements: 1988–1997." Western Centre for Economic Research, University of Alberta, Information Bulletin #49, 1998.

11. Norrie explained that the staple theory applied to the western Canadian regional economy but that, unlike those of earlier decades, the provincial governments of the 1970s and 1980s appropriated a much greater proportion of the economic rents. Norrie, "A Regional Economic Overview of the West Since 1945" in A. W. Rasporich, ed. *The Making of the Modern West: Western Canada Since 1945* (Calgary: University of Calgary Press 1984).

12. Editorial, *Globe and Mail* "Glen Clark's fishy attitude," 1 July 1998, A24; Glen Clark, "B.C. Premier Glen Clark: Fishing for the right deal" *Globe and Mail,* 24 March 1997, A19; Peter O'Neil, "Clark seeks federal aid for B.C. fishing towns" *Vancouver Sun* 3 April 1998, A4; treason is mentioned in Gordon Gibson "Oh for a solution to the slippery salmon" *Globe and Mail* 30 June 1998; the federal case is presented in David Anderson, "No pain, no gain: putting the fish first" *Vancouver Sun* 18 July 1998, A23.

13. These calculations appeared in a study by Chancellor Partners. It stated that forestry accounted for $18.6 billion in economic activity in 1996. The study was commissioned by the B.C. Forest Alliance and the Vancouver Board of Trade and released in March 1998; *Globe and Mail* 12 March 1998, B7.

14. Susan Smith, "B.C. resource sector feels Japan's economic slump," *Globe and Mail* 29 April 1998, B11. Smith notes that over half of Canada's $10.8 billion of commodity shipments to Japan in 1997 originated in B.C. Another $1 billion of these exports are in the form of bituminous coal.

15. Barrie McKenna, "Lumber legal battle looms" *Globe and Mail* 29 June 1998, B1; the 1970s discussions are noted in Gerald Friesen, *The Canadian Prairies: A History* (Toronto: University of Toronto Press, 1984).

16. Heather Scoffield, "Farmers fear rising subsidies: U.S.–EU schism escalating" *Globe and Mail* 25 May 1998, B1. The trade wars originated during the American Export Enhancement Program in the late 1980s and early 1990s and were renewed in 1993–4, when a one-year agreement put them to rest. They re-emerged in 1998.

17. Robert Matas, "B.C. activists learn colour of money" *Globe and Mail* 8 January 1996; Neal Hall, "4 environmentalists jailed 21 days over logging blockade" *Vancouver Sun* 4 April 1998, B3.

18. Michael Campbell, "More progressive moves like MacBlo's are necessary," *Vancouver Sun* 13 June 1998, A11; Steve Mertl, "Greenpeace celebrates as MacBlo to end clearcutting" *Edmonton Journal* 11 June 1998, A3. One possible next step is the issuance of eco-certification for wood products; "Firms looking for 'eco' label" and "British forest expert calls for certification" *Vancouver Sun* 3 April 1998, D2.

19. Andrew Nikiforuk, "Taking the axe to Alberta's forests: Economic development claims acreage as quickly as in Amazon rain forest" *Globe and Mail* 22 June 1998, A1, quoting a report written by Richard Thomas for Alberta's Environmental Protection Branch. The story declares: "Alberta's northern forest (half of the province) accounts for nearly one-tenth of Canada's great northern taiga—a fabled region that provides nearly $70 billion worth of free ecological services every year. These natural economies include oxygen-making, carbon-holding, fish-rearing, moose-making and water-cleaning as well as most of the world's fibre-growing."

20. Craig McInnes, "Tourism getting new respect in B.C." *Globe and Mail* 4 January 1996, A4.

21. John Carten, "Why B.C. should export fresh water" *Globe and Mail* 23 June 1998, A23.

22. Todd Hirsch, "The Western Economic Report Card: Performance and Outlooks in the New Global Economy" (Calgary: Canada West Foundation, November 1994). These calculations are based on Statistics Canada figures for 1993.

CHAPTER FOUR

Province-Building and the New Economy

THE WEST IS MORE than wheat, oil and forests. Indeed, in the decades after 1970, it became the home to many new forms of economic enterprise, including both government and private-sector activities. Partly due to new processing (shipping canola oil instead of canola seed, for example), the new economy also involved patriating the production of such knowledge-intensive goods as films and insurance and technological research. Combining the old resources and the new economy created a new kind of politics, one that has been described as province-building. This process, in turn, has added new dimensions to the Canadian federation. It sustains a common western economic perspective built on a single West and on four provincial economies that differ substantially in character and policy context.

I

UNTIL THE 1960s, AND despite some valiant efforts in Saskatchewan under the CCF, western governments had not discovered economic-diversification strategies that worked. In the 1970s, however, given the power of the state as a major employer and the extraordinary resource revenues available to the western provinces, provincial governments believed they possessed the ability to effect important changes in the economy. It is interesting to see that, by the 1990s, their strategies had changed considerably, but that the effects of a generation-long campaign to produce more diversified provinces were apparent everywhere.

In the decades after the Second World War, western political leaders seemed determined to effect changes in the community's reliance on primary resource exports. From the 1970s, they relied increasingly on growing business communities. Premiers Lougheed (Alberta) and Blakeney (Saskatchewan), in particular, provided the energy to effect a psychological shift in their administrations and, more broadly, in their provinces. Suddenly the prospect of mature and diversified *provincial* economies seemed within reach. Quebecers think of premiers Jean Lesage and Daniel Johnson in this context, New Brunswickers of Louis Robichaud, but the phenomenon was just as striking in the West.

The emergence of province-building as a project did not drastically reorient the historical trajectory of the western provinces. Resources remained king. But governments of every political stripe, in seeking to build provincial empires, recognized that they faced intractable international forces. They found opportunities for creativity in the spheres they controlled, notably health care and education, but also in the private sector.

What were these intractable forces that the western governments were learning to accommodate? One might reply that the premiers were becoming inured to the dominance of an international capitalist system. They were coming to terms with what was possible and what was beyond the reach of local governments, given the apparent strengths—indeed, the ascendancy—of the competitive market approach to organizing the world economy.

Before the 1970s, as Kenneth Norrie concluded, Prairie governments and their citizenry were still arguing about the consequences of Sir John A's first national policy. Of course people in both B.C. and the Prairies were also trying to mitigate the worst effects of this economic system by implementing the social welfare state that has been described as a second national policy.

Whether supporters or opponents of particular governments and policies, as Norrie has explained, westerners had struggled to understand and employ government's powers over the economy. Increasingly they were reaching the realization, he says, that

> the basic economic structure of the western economies is effectively explained by geography, history and market forces. The implication is that federal economic policies, with the possible exception of the Crow rate distortion, have played little

or no role in determining this structure. In particular, they have not made the West less industrialized
or diversified than it might have been otherwise.
This is not to say that some of these policies have
not reallocated income among regions within
Canada to the detriment of the West. Indeed they
have done this. . . .[1]

In other words, westerners came to see that while federal government favouritism for central Canada may have made Prairie residents poorer, it did not prevent western diversification. Therefore,
they concluded that the old debates about the national policy's effect
on the location of industry should be abandoned.

After 1980 western provincial premiers joined forces with their
colleagues from other provinces in seeking to use the powers they
had long possessed to greater economic effect. They believed that a
broader-based, more mature economy now was within their grasp, if
they could only choose wisely and build upon the creativity of their
own citizens. The old battles were coming to an end. New spheres,
equally likely to provoke conflict, were opening up. Ready or not,
Canada was embarking on the era of the third national economic
policy.

II

THE EMERGENCE OF THE manufacturing, service and information
economy in Canada occurred largely after the Second World War.
In 1921 about half of the western workforce could be described
as belonging to the secondary and tertiary sectors, and half to the
primary sector, chiefly in agriculture. These proportions were little
different in 1941. Yet in 1981 the proportions were eighty-six
percent (secondary and tertiary) and fourteen percent (primary).[2]
That trend has continued.

Nine in ten workers in western Canada are now in jobs associated with manufacturing, sales, transportation, clerical work, education, management and the trio of health, natural and social sciences.
Think of the provincial departments of education and school boards
as employers and all their teachers and support personnel as
workers; add all the workers in health care institutions; add all the
provincial and municipal employees and those among the federal
civil servants who live in the West; add the major publicly
owned corporations, such as the provincial telephone, automobile

insurance and electrical power enterprises; add the co-operatives and credit unions that serve the West, from the Federated Co-operative retail system to Vancouver City Savings (Credit Union) and Saskatchewan Credit Union Central; add the universities and publicly supported research institutions; add the publicly traded corporations with western headquarters, such as Great-West Life, Investors Group, Canwest Global Communications, Westfair Foods, ATCO Limited, Gendis, Loewen Group, the North West Company, Bentall, Shaw Communications, Moffat Communications, Western International Communications, New Flyer Bus, Western Star Trucks and Canadian Airlines International; finally, add the major privately held western corporations such as James Richardson, Palliser Furniture, Jim Pattison Group, PCL Construction and Loram. These corporations represent huge amounts of labour, investment and service; their futures are decided within western Canada; they are not merely confined to the production of unprocessed or primary products.

Manufacturing in Canada has historically been allocated to Ontario and Quebec and, to a much lesser degree, the Atlantic provinces. In western Canada, the value of manufacturing has always been seen as small relative to earnings in the farm and resource industries. Yet these generalizations are not borne out by the general pattern of manufacturing growth over the past generation. Western manufacturing has increased in this era and promises to grow in relative importance in the next decades.

Measured by its share of the value of all economic activity in Canada, manufacturing represents about one-sixth of Canada's gross domestic product. In western Canada, manufacturing constitutes a slightly smaller but still noteworthy share of GDP in British Columbia and Manitoba (about one-eighth in each case) and smaller proportions again in Alberta and Saskatchewan (about one-twentieth in each).[3] Though smaller than the national average, this western manufacturing is significant, especially because it provides a foundation for growth.

An Economic Council of Canada report concluded in the early 1980s that manufacturing was developing in the West simply because population increases and urban density offered the proper conditions for growth. The council's report declared:

> Our research on manufacturing in Manitoba suggests that some of the manufacturing [in two of

the province's leading industries—clothing and
transportation equipment] is there despite the
apparent locational disadvantages of distance and
small local market size. Some of us strongly
believe that this reflects the deeper reality that
successful manufacturing enterprises can be created by determined effort.[4]

The council opposed subsidies to individual firms and government
interventions to alter the course of economic development. Rather,
it stressed the role of non-business factors in determining location:

[T]hose starting the firms lived in Manitoba and
saw no reason to pull up roots and move elsewhere
before setting up business. Most of the firms were
long-established. . . . We conclude from all of this
that locational problems have probably been over-
estimated and the role of the entrepreneur underestimated in western manufacturing.[5]

There were occasions when eastern Canadian and Ottawa factors did influence western manufacturing firms. A case that received
much attention was the 1986 contest between Bristol Aerospace of
Winnipeg and Canadair of Montreal for the contract to maintain
the Canadian Armed Forces jet fighters, the CF-18s. The Winnipeg
firm's bid apparently won on both price and technical grounds. Bristol failed to secure the contract, however, because the federal government chose Canadair on the basis of other "national interest"
factors, none of which received much of a hearing in the subsequent
uproar about political favouritism. Preston Manning's decision to
launch the Reform Party was taken after this wave of protest washed
over western Canada.[6]

As the CF-18 story illustrates, government contracts, often
involving millions of dollars, do shape industrial decisions and the
larger community. An economic success story in British Columbia
during the 1990s was MacDonald Dettwiler and Associates Ltd. of
Richmond, a homegrown high-technology firm. The company
developed computer applications for cartography, geological
exploration and special kinds of surveillance, notably environmental monitoring of forests, crops and oceans. In 1998 it employed
nine hundred workers and had won a $300 million contract to
build a radar satellite for the Canadian Space Agency, as well as a

$100 million contract to reorganize the British Columbia government's electronic data-management services. Significantly, given all the talk of private enterprise such innovative firms inspire, much of its work was based on government contracts.[7]

Creo Products offers an interesting parallel. This Vancouver firm developed computer-to-plate printing systems in the 1980s. It soon won numerous technology awards because the innovation cut out costly steps in the printing process. The system permitted the direct transfer of computer-generated images and text onto light-sensitive or heat-sensitive plates using laser beams. Film was eliminated, production time reduced and resolution enhanced, while the entire process was more environmentally friendly because the metal contaminants associated with film were gone. By the mid-1990s, Creo employed over nine hundred workers worldwide and had invested millions of dollars in research and product development.

A similar story, but in energy rather than imaging technology, may take place at Ballard Power Systems of Vancouver. There, the search for alternative energy sources led a team of engineers to stack fuel cell plates (a carbon plate, a platinum catalyst and an electrolyte membrane) that convert hydrogen or natural gas into electricity. In 1997 alone the firm signed $1 billion in deals with Ford, Daimler-Benz and GEC Alsthom for the development of this fuel cell technology. In this case, the product is a little farther from market than Creo's printing system and the impact on the local workforce harder to foresee, but its potential relevance to the manufacturing sector is unmistakable.[8]

Similar cases can be found in each of the western provinces. In Edmonton a computer program for playing checkers contributed to DNA research. Interestingly, the firm Biotools, producer of the software originally designed to win at checkers, adapted it to facilitate manipulation of vast amounts of genetic data. This research was sustained by the offspring of Alberta oil revenues, the Heritage Fund. The Lougheed government set up a $300 million trust (now worth $800 million) to attract medical researchers and, thereby, to diversify the economy in just the sorts of venture—biomedical engineering and diabetes research—that have since developed.[9] Calgary's research and development authority claims that the value of production in advanced technology (perhaps a fuzzy category) "tripled in the past decade to $4.6 billion, while direct employment has doubled to more than 26,000."[10] Such anecdotes serve best as illustrations of changes in the advanced economies, not uniquely in western Canada. A Statistics Canada study of high-technology work concluded that jobs for computer programmers and systems analysts doubled in number from late 1992 to late 1997 to more than a quarter million (267,000), but that western Canada's proportion of the total did not nearly match that of Ontario and Quebec.[11] Nonetheless, the many success stories in western Canadian manufacturing suggest that economic diversification is proceeding apace.

These few examples, and there are many more, illustrate how new manufacturing finds its support in both the private and public sectors and its roots where accidents of location and entrepreneurial ambition happen to occur. Western Canada has been the beneficiary of some of these coincidences, sufficient to generate an atmosphere of growth in Alberta and British Columbia, and also, though to a lesser degree, in Manitoba and Saskatchewan.

I I I

THE SERVICE SECTOR AND the enterprises associated with communications also offer many examples of economic enterprise. Vancouver's film industry, complete with the rain that allegedly sent "The X-Files" packing and that gives it the unwanted title "brollywood," has been booming for a decade. It generated $630 million in economic activity in 1997. Manitoba, long the scene of alternative screen work, is now offering sufficiently attractive tax credits that an industry of $500,000 a year in 1988 is expected to produce $40 million of economic activity and the equivalent of 1,100 job-years in 1998.[12]

Communications corporations have been making headlines in the 1990s. Three of them, Canwest Global (Manitoba), Western International Communications (British Columbia) and Shaw Communications (Alberta), were locked in a dramatic financial struggle during 1997–98. These corporations own television and radio stations, pay-TV and specialty channels, and are moving into the business of program production. The two survivors in their ownership struggle, Shaw and Canwest, can be fairly described as billion-dollar enterprises, in terms of capitalization and revenue.[13]

As in other parts of the world, much of this new economy is located in the West's metropolitan centres. This is not, however, the only site of economic change. Many of the West's smaller cities— Medicine Hat, Nanaimo, Red Deer, Chiliwack, Prince Albert, Brandon—appear near the top of the list of Canadian urban centres with the greatest job growth in the past three years.[14]

The same trend has been discerned in certain favoured rural areas, usually those within hailing distance of a metropolis. In Alberta, where population growth has been rapid, certain rural census districts have grown more rapidly than the province as a whole between 1991 and 1996. This rural growth has been attributed to advances in communications technology that permit business services to be supplied by telecommuters who prefer rural life.[15]

The old truths about western Canadian resource exports remain true, despite these changes in the secondary and tertiary sectors. Alberta's economy is a little more balanced today, but the price of oil and gas are still crucial preoccupations for its citizens. British Columbia has some high-technology firms, but they account for only three percent of the provincial economic output, compared to tourism's five percent and forestry's twenty percent. Saskatchewan is still a primary export economy. Only Manitoba has the kind of diversification one might describe as balanced. Western Canada remains a resource-producing, primary-goods-exporting economy. As compared to forty or even just ten years ago, however, it has growing enterprises in manufacturing, communications and the so-called knowledge-intensive industries. Based in cities, for the most part, and often subject to provincial policies, many of these industries were also concentrated in the cultural and knowledge-based activities, such as local television, that had a provincial profile. The businesses and their leaders contributed to a province-building ethos even as they operated within an increasingly global market and network of relationships.

REFERENCES

1. Kenneth H. Norrie, "A Regional Economic Overview of the West Since 1945" in A.W. Rasporich, ed. *The Making of the Modern West: Western Canada Since 1945* (Calgary: University of Calgary Press 1984) pp. 75–6.

2. Economic Council of Canada, *Western Transition* (Ottawa: Supply and Services Canada 1984) pp. 14–18, Tables 2–11, 2–12, based on data from Statistics Canada and on B.R. Blishen and H.A. McRoberts, "A Revised Socioeconomic Index for Occupations in Canada" in *Canadian Review of Sociology and Anthropology* 13, 1 (1976).

3. Cy Gonick, "The Manitoba Economy Since World War II" in James Silver and Jeremy Hull, eds. *The Political Economy of Manitoba* (Regina: Canadian Plains Research Centre 1990) p. 40.

4. Economic Council of Canada, *Western Transition* (Ottawa: Supply and Services Canada 1984) p. 187. The council added: "We think the local business community needs to make the effort, in collaboration with provincial and municipal governments, to develop manufacturing industries. We do not have subsidies in mind; rather, we are convinced that a canvass of local capabilities and potentialities would lead to successful initiatives in manufacturing."

5. *Western Transition* pp. 188–9.

6. Tom Flanagan, *Waiting for the Wave: The Reform Party and Preston Manning* (Toronto: Stoddart 1995) p. 39; Jeffrey Simpson, *Faultlines: Struggling for a Canadian Vision* (Toronto: Harper Collins 1993) pp. 107–114.

7. The MacDonald Dettwiler story can be followed in the *Vancouver Sun*: 27 March 1996, A33; 5 September 1996, C1; 6 November 1996, D7; 13 January 1997, D1; 28 February 1998, E1; 12 March 1998, D4; also Ann Gibbon, "B.C. government selling OnLine data base: province trying to give high-tech sector a push" *Globe and Mail* 25 July 1998, B4.

8. Keith Damsell, "With $2.5B in expectations, what's next at the Next Big Thing?" *Financial Post* 2 January 1998; doubts were raised in Barbara Aarsteinsen, "Stock split elevates Ballard shares" *Vancouver Sun* 4 April 1998, D1; but positive reports appeared in Ann Gibbon, "Ballard powers up for production" *Globe and Mail* 17 August 1998, B11. This report was buoyed by the announcement that Ballard had delivered a fuel cell to Ford.

9. Brian Laghi, "The bright idea with a checkers past: With provincial help, a computer game has graduated into a tool for medical research" *Globe and Mail* 23 October 1997, A2.

10. Brian Laghi, "Calgary reaps a renaissance: Recovery of oil industry, newfound political clout make city a formidable power" *Globe and Mail* 3 January 1996, A1; similarly, a Vancouver story claimed that high-tech industries were growing at the rate of twenty-two percent annually in B.C. and represented revenue of $7.6 billion in 1997. The story claimed that ninety percent of this activity took place in the Vancouver area; Catherine Porter, "For a real good time, join a high-tech firm" *Vancouver Sun* 1 August 1998, A1,7.

11. Patrick Brethour, "High-tech skills keeping pace with computer job boom" *Globe and Mail* 11 June 1998, B1.

12. Murray McNeill, "Manitoba tax credit gets star billing: provincial program provides boost to already burgeoning film industry" *Winnipeg Free Press* 16 April 1998; Ann Gibbon, "Rising stars improve economic picture" *Globe and Mail* 21 March 1998, A6.

13. Robert Brehl, "The scramble for WIC" *Globe and Mail* 28 March 1998, B1; Janet McFarland, "CanWest leaps ahead of CTV," and Gayle MacDonald and Doug Saunders, "CanWest-Shaw swap re-jigs broadcast market" *Globe and Mail* 19 August 1998, A1, B1.

14. Bruce Little, "Smaller cities with big job gains" *Globe and Mail* 6 April 1998, A5.

15. Edward J. Chambers and Mae Deans, "The Rural Renaissance in Alberta: Some Empirical Evidence" University of Alberta Western Centre for Economic Research *Information Bulletin* 50 (May 1998); the trend is anticipated in Graham F. Parsons, "Electronic By-ways: Information and Services in the New Rural West" Canada West Foundation, May 1995.

CHAPTER FIVE

The Aboriginal Past

THEIR ODYSSEY IS AS long and varied as that of any people in the world. Their profound role in shaping a distinctive Canadian vision in human affairs makes them central to today's national society. Yet other Canadians often do not see the significance of this aboriginal presence.

Westerners, above all other Canadians except residents of the north, have learned in recent years that First Nations people are taking on new roles. Because aboriginal matters are near the top of the social and political agenda in western Canada today, an understanding of aboriginal–Canada relations—how we got to where we are today—has become a western preoccupation that might surprise the rest of the country. I say this recognizing that the battles in Quebec at Oka and the Mercier bridge, in Ontario and New Brunswick, in Nova Scotia and Labrador demonstrate the transcontinental reach of aboriginal issues.

I

CANADA'S ABORIGINAL PEOPLE NUMBER about one million. Given the shortcomings of the census on Indian reserves and in the urban diaspora, and the difficulties of measuring such self-identifications as Métis status, they have been undercounted in official records, but they constitute about three percent of the total population.

Only Ontario among the eastern Canadian provinces has a number of aboriginal residents that approaches the aboriginal population in each of the western provinces. However, given its larger total population, First Nations citizens make up a much smaller fraction of the Ontario society and public consciousness. It is noteworthy that the proportion of aboriginal people in each of the six eastern provinces is less than the national average—that is, under two percent.[1]

In western Canada, the aboriginal presence in the community is much greater. There are over 100,000 First Nations people in each of the four western provinces, comprising nearly ten percent of the regional population, as well as many thousands of Métis.

Imagine working in a community where one in eight people (Manitoba and Saskatchewan), or one in fifteen (Alberta and British Columbia) is aboriginal. This is roughly the size of the African-American fraction in the United States. For reasons of its poverty alone, it demands attention.

When an experienced Quebec journalist, Gérald LeBlanc of *La Presse*, visited Winnipeg, he was struck by a "dramatic situation . . . an impression of desolation" in the aboriginal neighbourhoods. He spoke to a number of community leaders and concluded, "If Manitoba represents the way of the future for Canada's aboriginal people, Winnipeg is also a time bomb that must be quickly disarmed."[2] The same observation could be made of Regina, Saskatoon, Prince Albert, Edmonton and a number of reserve communities.

II

UNDERSTAND THE ABORIGINAL POINT of view. Native Canadians have lived here from time immemorial. This is the only place on earth they call home. Whether First Nations, Métis or Inuit, their sense of belonging is tied firmly to this particular place by thousands of years of experience.

What we make of this long, continuous presence here is up to us as a community. Aboriginal people insist that the exceptional length of their presence in this land be acknowledged by their fellow citizens.

Indeed, this is what happened when Canadians debated the rewriting of the Constitution in the late 1970s and early 1980s. As a result of aboriginal contributions to the discussion, a section was added to the Charter of Rights and Freedoms that recognizes the "existing treaty and Aboriginal rights of the Indian, Inuit, and Métis peoples of Canada." It is left to Canadians, therefore, to decide what those existing rights are.

The historian Olive Dickason, who is herself Métis and grew up in an aboriginal community, puts the case for an aboriginal perspective on the Canadian past in her sweeping volume *Canada's First Nations*. She writes that, even at the moment of their beginnings, when their identity with Asia was clearest, the peoples of the Americas were developing distinct perspectives that extended across the entire hemisphere from the Arctic to the Cape of Good Hope. Within just a few generations they constituted a civilization, and their achievements could be spoken of in the same way one might describe the empires created by the Han of China, the Gupta of India, the imperial figures of Africa, or the Hellenic people of the Mediterranean.[3]

III

THE EXPERIENCE OF ABORIGINAL people in their relations with newcomers in northern North America differed from region to region. Western and northern Canada, last to feel the full impact of European trade, religions and diseases, avoided the sudden tragedies that destroyed the Beothuk, decimated the Atlantic coastal peoples, introduced guns to the Huron–Iroquois conflicts on the St. Lawrence and left only a few thousand survivors in eastern Canada by the opening of the nineteenth century.

Instead, the western fur trade evolved slowly and relatively peacefully over several centuries. As guests on the rim of the aboriginal universe, the traders gradually introduced European notions of price, market and wage while conveying new technologies, new attitudes to gender and work, and new priorities for diplomacy. The consequence is a shared past of economic and political co-operation between aboriginal and European Canadians that still, after a century of mistakes, carries significant purpose and lasting value.

Crucial errors occurred, nevertheless, during the West's transition to Canadian rule. Confederation (1867), annexation of the North-West (1870) and British Columbia's adhesion to Canada (1871) took place in a brief period of intense political activity. Rules inherited from Great Britain had previously governed relations with aboriginal people. These laws envisaged the gradual dispossession and eventual "civilizing" of the First Nations—meaning their "Europeanizing." Responsibility for the vast western half of the continent, however, weighed heavily on Canadian shoulders, and fears of aboriginal–white violence, such as that threatened in Red River in 1869–70, concerned the political leaders. The Minnesota wars of the 1860s—not to mention the racial conflicts elsewhere in the British Empire—spurred the nation-builders to take an aggressive approach to aboriginal control. The decisions taken in the late nineteenth century have not served Canadians well.

The most notable result, from the aboriginal vantage point, was the creation of three Wests. First, the Prairies were ceded to Canada by treaties signed by aboriginal leaders on behalf of all their followers. The aboriginal people covered by the treaties represent a distinct group of western Canadian citizens. Second, the claims of most First Nations in British Columbia were never settled. Because aboriginal sovereignty was not relinquished, the governments and people of B.C. now face, at the opening of the twenty-first century, the onerous task of deciding how to come to terms with that pivotal constitutional phrase "existing aboriginal rights." Most of the First Nations people of British Columbia fall into this second category of aboriginal citizen. Third, the Métis belonged to neither of the above camps. They did not have treaties, but they did undertake acts of military resistance, in Manitoba in 1869–70, and in the North-West Territories in 1885. After the battle at Batoche and the execution of Louis Riel, they were left on the margins of both First Nations and European Canadian communities, their status unresolved from that day to this, except for an Alberta settlement regime and recent Saskatchewan attempts to establish an official census.

The Prairie treaties provided a measure of peace for First Nations people and a framework for continuing relations. They also preserved the idea that two parties—two types of nation—had negotiated an understanding. The aboriginal people gave up a degree of sovereignty; Canada acknowledged that the First Nations—but not necessarily the Métis—had previously possessed sovereignty. Canada also accepted responsibility for the aboriginal condition in the future.

Treaties aside, the Native Canadians of western Canada endured a century of determined and unsuccessful assimilation efforts by government, church and police officials. The pivotal decision, an act passed by the federal government near the start of this period, deliberately circumvented and circumscribed the treaty process. By this Indian Act of 1876—amended many times in the intervening years, including a reassessment in 1951 that changed very little—aboriginal people lost control over their own affairs.

By amendments around the turn of the century, even rituals and customs central to their religions were outlawed on pain of imprisonment.

In another long-term policy, the government took increasing numbers of aboriginal children from their parents and placed them in church-run residential schools. In the best circumstances, children acquired literacy and language skills and some training in trade and agriculture. Most schools, however, were incubators of disease, factories for child labour and sometimes homes of horrible abuse. In retrospect, the government's decision to assume control of these children and to usurp the parents' authority was a fundamental choice with multigenerational consequences.[4]

In the simpler economies of the nineteenth century, aboriginal people lived in a manner common to many households on Canada's frontiers. They sought wage labour as domestic servants and casual farmhands, worked in construction, freighting and canning jobs, and farmed and trapped and fished and hunted. This sufficed until, during the first half of the twentieth century, the margins of the old economy shrank and the boundaries of the new expanded, leaving little opportunity and fewer resources for those who still possessed traditional skills but were less equipped to deal with the demands of international capital.

After 1945 a worldwide renaissance of colonized peoples raised the hopes of western Canada's aboriginal leaders. Their own political campaigns during the interwar years and their peoples' effective contributions to Canada's war effort fuelled a pan-Canadian First Nations resistance movement. When Jean Chrétien unveiled the White Paper on Indian policy in 1969, calling for the end of a distinct aboriginal category of citizenship, he was met by a storm of protest that had been brewing for decades.

A less dramatic but equally important turning point involved Joseph Drybones. A middle-aged Dene man, Joseph was arrested in the Old Stope tavern in Yellowknife by the Royal Canadian Mounted Police in 1967 on the charge that he had contravened a section of the Indian Act by being intoxicated and by drinking off the reserve—though there were then no reserves in the Northwest Territories. Had he been white, Joseph would have faced a lesser sentence and certainly would have been permitted to imbibe a little alcohol. Noting the conflict between Canada's Bill of Rights and the Indian Act, the judge acquitted him. The Supreme Court justices concurred with this decision. Henceforth, the laws affecting aboriginal people, including the Indian Act, would have to conform to the standards that governed laws affecting other Canadians.[5]

During the 1960s and 1970s Aboriginal people were finally recognized as full citizens of Canada. Their Prairie treaties, which had been negotiated between the Crown and the chiefs and therefore were part of the country's constitutional arrangements, henceforth would ensure that relations between government and these particular aboriginal people, though always uneasy, would be framed by commonly understood principles of law and politics. The absence of treaties in British Columbia was a source of thornier problems. Their greater proportion of the population in the western provinces guaranteed that aboriginal peoples' relations with the larger community would be especially pressing in that section of the country. The Métis largely remained outside this particular debate. Only their continuing struggle for recognition of their land claims and their inclusion in the 1982 Constitution put Métis status on the agenda of the Canadian people. In the future Canadians would have to learn a great deal more about these issues and to exercise a patience to match that of aboriginal people in the preceding century.[6]

The implications for western Canada of these Aboriginal issues included ownership of natural resources and tracts of land, race relations in every community, the pressing economic questions associated with poverty in both reserve and city, the training of future members of the workforce, and the alienation of aboriginal young people, expressed in gangs and crime. Though these are pan-Canadian issues, of course, but their significance is greater in the West for one obvious reason: the central role of aboriginal people in each western province places their concerns at the forefront of every citizen's consciousness.

REFERENCES

1. The highest proportions of aboriginal people in these populations are in the Yukon (nearly twenty percent) and Northwest Territories (nearly sixty percent). One recent study of these population numbers is Mary Jane Norris, Don Kerr, François Nault, "Projections of the Population with Aboriginal Identity, Canada, 1991–2016: Summary Report," Canada Mortgage and Housing Corporation project for the Royal Commission on Aboriginal Peoples, 1996.

2. Gérald LeBlanc, "50 000 autochtones croupissent à Winnipeg." *La Presse* 18 May 1996.

3. Olive Dickason, *Canada's First Nations: A History of Founding Peoples from Earliest Times* (Toronto: Oxford University Press 1997, 2nd ed.) pp. 41–2, citing Joseph Needham and Lu Gwei-Djen, *Trans-Pacific Echoes and Resonances: Listening Once Again* (Singapore and Philadelphia 1985) pp. 62–3; see, for example, Linda Schele and David Freidel, *A Forest of Kings: The Untold Story of the Ancient Maya* (New York 1990) and Michael D. Coe, *Breaking the Maya Code* (London 1992).

4. John S. Milloy, *'A National Crime': The Canadian Government and the Residential School System, 1879 to 1986* (Winnipeg: University of Manitoba Press 1999).

5. Stephen Hume, "Justice served over a drink" in the *Vancouver Sun* 4 April 1998, G4.

6. A recent survey of this story is Arthur J. Ray, *I Have Lived Here Since the World Began: An Illustrated History of Canada's Native People* (Toronto: Key Porter Books, Lester Publishing 1996); another is James R. Miller, *Skyscrapers Hide the Heavens: A History of Indian–White Relations in Canada* (Toronto: University of Toronto Press 1989) and a third is the work by Olive Dickason cited above.

CHAPTER SIX

Historic Grievances
in an Immigrant Society

MANY NORTH AMERICAN COMMUNITIES have had to deal with race relations and immigration during their history. Western Canada, certainly, should be counted as one that has experienced many intense ethnic conflicts. Nonetheless, it would be wrong to argue that the region was exceptionally burdened by racism or interracial battles. As in the case of aboriginal people, in the matter of immigrants' relations with the dominant culture, the circumstances in western Canadian differ from those in other parts of the country.

If anything, the western Canadian social reality has been so diverse for so many years that it constitutes an object lesson in individual and group accommodation. The stories of battles fought—and eventually won—are now part of western communities' identities.

I

THE FIRST RACIAL DEBATES in western Canada occurred in the early nineteenth century. During several centuries of the fur trade, in which many European–aboriginal partnerships were forged, new mixed-race communities known today as the Métis developed. However, relations between races were made more difficult by conflicts between business enterprises, those of France and England before 1760 and of the Hudson's Bay Company and the North-West Company from the 1780s to 1821. Indeed, the fiercest battles in western Canada in the early nineteenth century saw both Scots and Métis attach their "national" loyalties to the loyalty they owed their corporate partners. Thus, Métis and Nor'Westers, many of whom had Scottish connections, opposed the Hudson's Bay Company and its Scottish settlement at Red River in the Battle of Seven Oaks in 1816.

The tension in eastern Canada between French and English, Roman Catholic and Protestant, Ulster and Ireland, lowland and highland Scot, became a part of western Canadian experience in the second half of the nineteenth century. The Manitoba school question, one of the notorious constitutional struggles in the generation after Confederation, fell exactly along this divide. Protestants generally favoured a single, state-run public school; Catholics preferred a dual system—separate but equal—in which they could administer their own confessional schools. A Manitoba compromise, necessitated by five years of court cases, by a ruling of the Judicial Committee of the Privy Council in Great Britain (then Canada's highest court) and by an Ottawa intervention "remedying" the province's school law was arranged in 1897. It permitted a distinct Roman Catholic school system but required its supporters to pay twice for schools, once (voluntarily) for their own and a second time as part of the general taxes of the province.

The compromise in Saskatchewan and Alberta, reached when these provinces were created in 1905, permitted taxpayers to belong to *either* the "public" (usually Protestant), or the "separate" (usually Catholic) school district and required them to pay for only one system. The deal drove Clifford Sifton, a Manitoban and the negotiator of the 1897 compromise, from Prime Minister Laurier's cabinet, but it did hold firm during subsequent generations.

These schools questions were bitter public battles, fought as if the result would endure for a millennium. They reflected inherited hostilities in the community, prejudices that had been burnished in Europe and the United States as well as in eastern Canada. One should note, however, that working relations were eventually established among the camps of school supporters in each of western Canada's provincial communities.

Western Canada's social relations became much more complicated, and significantly different from those in eastern Canada, around the turn of the twentieth century. The change was caused by the extraordinary wave of immigration that transformed the Prairies during the first three decades of the century. The older society was inundated with newcomers, including a substantial number who were neither English nor French but rather from other parts of Europe. British Columbia also received noteworthy numbers of immigrants, among whom those of Chinese, Japanese and South Asian (what is now India and Pakistan) origin caused the greatest stir. In both the Prairies and British Columbia, the presence of the newcomers challenged the recently established consensus that favoured the Protestant, English-speaking majority.

Manitoba again was the crucible of racial tensions in this era, partly because the schools compromise of 1897 was worded loosely—and perhaps was deliberately ambiguous. The phrase that caused so much tension between British Canadians and new European arrivals in the province guaranteed instruction in English and "another language on a bilingual basis." Within the space of a few years, schools and even teacher training existed in French, German, Ukrainian and Polish. By the outbreak of the First World War in 1914, this "bilingualism" was perceived by many British-Canadian leaders to be a threat to social harmony. Could these hyphenated Canadians not appreciate, they asked, that they were expected to melt into the majority?

Concessions to the languages of the newcomers were repealed in each Prairie province between 1912 and 1917. Henceforth, except in some French communities where school superintendents looked the other way, the language of instruction was exclusively English.

Racial tensions rose and fell during the first half of the twentieth century but never disappeared completely. Several thousand Mennonites left Manitoba after 1917 because they could not accept the school law revisions. Ukrainians perceived the wartime internment of five thousand men from their community as a political betrayal and a racial slight; this wound has never been forgotten. The bitter denunciation of Germans—"Huns"—during the war similarly required two decades to bury and then was revived by the Second World War. Anti-Asian laws, especially in British Columbia but also in the Prairie provinces, erected walls between the communities that seemed at the time to be nearly insurmountable. Jews endured restrictive codes both in land purchases and in university registration.

The rise of the Ku Klux Klan, notably in Saskatchewan during the 1920s, illustrated the seriousness of racial differences. Burning crosses as a warning to Roman Catholics, vicious abuse of Eastern Europeans and calls for the cessation of Asian immigration must put the lie to any romantic notion that Canadians have been somehow immune to the virus of race hatred. Even the most generous responses to immigrants were predicated on the assumption that rapid assimilation must occur, whether through education of the

foreigner (the solution proposed by educator and later Saskatchewan Premier J.T.M. Anderson), or by means of solemn patience
and respect (as author Robert England proposed).

The mass immigration of the early twentieth century imposed
greater burdens on Canadian public policy. The newcomers to western Canada did not know the rest of the country. They had arrived
at Pacific or Atlantic ports and been conveyed directly, with scarcely
a pause, to the district in which they now lived. Families grew up
without contact with the larger Canada and, at times, precious little
connection to their homelands.

According to the 1931 census, a distinctive plural society had
taken shape in the west. One-third of all residents had been born
outside Canada. Of these, half had been born in the British Isles,
one-fifth in eastern (and southern) Europe, and one-fifth in western
(and northern) Europe. By the early 1940s this generalization could
be applied to the ethnic composition of the Prairies: half British,
one-fifth eastern and southern European, one-fifth western and
northern. Aboriginal people, hit hard by starvation, tuberculosis and
other diseases of poverty, accounted for less than one-tenth of the
total and were not to see the stabilization of their numbers for
another decade.

Had a kind of compromise been struck in western Canada, a
deal in which each ethnic subcommunity accepted the principle of
live and let live? Though the idea contains a broad truth, it is not
entirely accurate. There has never been a period when these
conflicts among different cultural groups have not been simmering.

The deepest hostility was that expressed by European Canadians
in British Columbia towards Asian immigrants. Chinese workers had
arrived in the province during the closing decades of the nineteenth
century, paid a special immigration fee (the so-called "head tax") to
enter the country and then accepted some of the roughest and most
dangerous work assignments, in the expectation that they would be
able to send money to their impoverished families in southern China.
The waves of Asian newcomers to Canada ended with the Chinese
Immigration Act of 1923 and a 1928 quota on Japanese immigration,
laws that remained in place until the issue was revisited after the
Second World War. Chinese and Japanese Canadians gained the federal franchise only in 1947 and 1949 respectively.

The Japanese faced the most extraordinary disruption. Shortly
after Pearl Harbour, the Canadian government, driven by per-
fervid British Columbia opinion, resolved to disperse the large

Japanese Canadian communities on the Pacific coast and to confiscate individual holdings, even though seventy-five percent of the affected people were Canadian nationals and no evidence of trouble had surfaced. Having taken their property and sources of income, which provoked great struggles for proper compensation after 1945, the government dispatched the Japanese Canadian families eastward. Many ended up in inadequate camps in the interior of the province or on sugar beet farms in southern Alberta and southern Manitoba. The evacuation and property confiscation constituted a profound denial of their civil rights. Japanese Canadians sought an official apology for an entire generation and were finally successful in the 1980s. Nevertheless, that community will never forget the government's original action.

Another wave of European-origin immigrants after the Second World War, between roughly 1947 and the mid-1960s, reinforced consciousness of European ethnic identity in many communities—German, Ukrainian, Polish, Czech, Jewish and English. Sustaining their distinct ethnic characteristics became a preoccupation of many. Some families concentrated on dance, many laboured long hours to teach a language or to embed knowledge about special foods and festival customs (Christmas and Easter, for example) in their children, and many paid close attention to church attendance and matters of faith. Many also belonged to associations that carried their colours into sports leagues and cultural events.

The most publicized ethnic struggle in the decade after the war was the accommodation of these postwar refugees. No sooner was this issue more or less quiet than the nationwide debate over the status of French as an official language burst into public prominence. The Royal Commission on Bilingualism and Biculturalism, appointed in 1963, discovered in its hearings in western Canada that many communities were unwilling to countenance special privileges, as it was put, for any citizen. These Ukrainians and Germans and Swedes had given up their languages in favour of English, the universal language of the country and the continent, as they saw it; why should the French, now a small minority in each western province, receive special grants and school programs and government services?

The commissioners eventually devoted a special volume of their report to *The Cultural Contribution of the Other Ethnic Groups.* The Trudeau government responded by launching a new government program on "multiculturalism" in 1971. This policy focused on the ethnic communities' concerns to ensure a degree of cultural retention among their members. It also promised to respect the communities' own priorities for programs on integration and education.[1]

The policy was greeted with enthusiasm among ethnic groups in western Canada. It seemed to provide national recognition, however belated, for a "third force," neither English nor French, as an important component of Canada. Indeed, the simultaneous popularity of "mosaic" as a depiction of Canada gave evidence of a widespread view.

Contrasts between Canada's tolerance of ethnic cultural retention and an alleged melting pot in the United States became common in these years. They were part of a brief moment of multicultural celebration. However, seventy-five years of tensions over immigration policy and the mixing of races, as well as a century of struggles between Roman Catholics and Protestants, could not be ignored. Western Canada entered the last quarter of the twentieth century having witnessed much unease among its many cultural communities. Alternatively, one might say that most of the one-time persecuted (though not all) remained in the West, having coped with the hostility and having established more amicable relations with the rest of the community. They lived side by side in suburbs, consumed the same goods and travelled to the same vacation spots.

Had the larger society in this part of Canada acquired a degree of tolerance on just these issues of race and immigration? Or did it merely exhibit a greater nervousness when slights occurred? Or—a third possibility—had it become so firmly assimilationist that it expressed greater determination to erase ethnic differences? My reaction to such questions is that they merely elaborate on the obvious: yes, there is considerable awareness of race and ethnic mixing in western Canada; yes, the West has seen racist words and even violent racial conflict; and yes, there is a strong strain of assimilationism in western Canadian communities, especially those that have been most thoroughly integrated into a Canadian and North American, English-speaking model.

Taken together, too, the forces that have been discussed in the preceding chapters, including the long history of ethnic adaptations, the aboriginal numerical proportion and political importance, the noteworthy changes in urban economies and the drastic changes in rural resource economies, underline the eclipse of the old two-region notion of the West. Rather than Prairies and Coast, one can better appreciate why two alternative types of territorial identity, the single West and the four provinces, now seem more influential in Canadian life.

REFERENCES

1. Greg Gauld, "Multiculturalism: The Real Thing" in Stella Hryniuk, ed., *Twenty Years of Multiculturalism: Successes and Failures* (Winnipeg: St. John's College Press, 1992) pp. 9–16.

Part II

The Four Provinces Today

CHAPTER SEVEN

British Columbia

BRITISH COLUMBIA IS THE largest western province. Though slightly smaller in area and population than Quebec and Ontario, it has emerged in recent years as a third force in Confederation. Its metropolis, Vancouver, is certainly the most prominent urban centre west of Toronto. The lower mainland, for which Vancouver serves as the urban core, has boomed for more than a decade and now, with a population of nearly two million, accounts for greater than half the provincial population. There are two other populous central places in the province—the Victoria district on Vancouver Island and the Kelowna district in the Interior. They, too, have been coping with rapid growth. Though the province is undergoing an economic slowdown at the end of the 1990s, ten years of sustained growth have marked it as a favoured centre for the young and the upwardly mobile.

I

BRITISH COLUMBIA IS A very large, diverse and divided province, nearly half as large again in territory as any of the other three western provinces. The coast's high peaks and narrow fjords, and the tree-covered slopes in the Interior make for spectacular scenery. For purposes of description it is often divided into ten districts: the lower mainland, Vancouver Island, the Okanagan/Boundary, the two Kootenays (East and West) and five districts for the sparsely populated centre and north. As is often said, it is a sea of mountains.

It is composed of valleys and plateaus and numerous ranges of
mountains, including the Coast range, the Rockies and several
intermediate ranges. (The Columbia range, better known as
the Purcell, Selkirk, Monashee and Cariboo mountains, and the
Cassiar-Omineca range are both in the Interior, and a third,
the Insular range, extends northward from the United States to
Vancouver Island.)

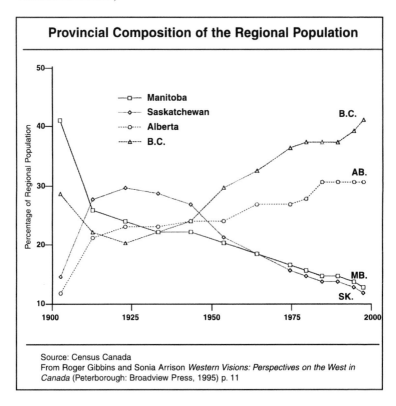

Provincial Composition of the Regional Population

Source: Census Canada
From Roger Gibbins and Sonia Arrison *Western Visions: Perspectives on the West in
Canada* (Peterborough: Broadview Press, 1995) p. 11

   The province's proportion of western Canada's population has
risen steadily from the mid-1920s, when it constituted about twenty
percent, to the present when it is over forty percent. The increase
during the 1980s and 1990s has been particularly marked.
   To visitors from other, slower cities, Vancouver represents
youth. Every second citizen in the downtown waterfront neighbourhoods seems to be pursuing or talking about physical fitness. If
the exercise session is over, they are heading for some vigorous, or

langorous, debate at one of the coffee shops that have proliferated
seemingly overnight. Vancouver offers a vibrant mixture of Asia
and Europe that is distinctively Pacific North American. Its setting
is much praised. Its density of population makes it western
Canada's most urban society. This concentration contrasts with the
other western Canadian cities, even though, like them, the lower
mainland relies on the automobile and now sprawls across miles of
suburbs, one developer-named "village" after another.

The Pacific shore defines the metropolis. The humid fir and
cedar forests of Stanley Park and the University of British Columbia endowment lands, the Lion's Gate bridge framed against the
mountains rising from the city's north shore, the ocean inlets and
arms and the Fraser River delta all suggest that this is a site shaped
by the relation between mainland and ocean.

Victoria is quieter, if only in contrast to Vancouver, and seems
to represent governmental caution, administrative reticence and
tourist gentility. I would mention the elderly who are said to have
flocked there from the rest of Canada, but residents of Victoria
would not look kindly on such generalizations. They insist that their
city is more than gardens and golf, that high tea at the Empress
Hotel is mainly for visitors, that its gentle climate enables Victori-
ans to be just as active as Lower mainlanders, and that they, too, are
vigorously pursuing some main chance. Those knitters and readers
on the coastal ferries must be wintering or on holiday. Indeed, a
recent analysis of the 1991–96 census period demonstrated that
young adults, not senior citizens, are most likely to move to B.C.
from other parts of Canada. A wave of migrating seniors did arrive
in the 1950s, chiefly from the Prairies, but has not been repeated in
recent decades.[1] And the presence of important Canadian military
installations and a growing concern about drug abuse put the lie to
talk of somnolence.

The burgeoning district of the Okanagan constitutes a third
metropolitan centre, though the three old towns at its heart—Ver-
non, Kelowna and Penticton—might seem too small to sustain such
a title. The three towns, situated in the middle and at the ends of
Okanagan Lake, constitute a chain of settlement with 300,000 residents (half in the Kelowna region alone) and are growing faster than
any other part of western Canada with the exception of a few of the
lower mainland municipalities. Its situation—mild climate, the lake
itself, the skiing and vineyards and golf courses—suggests that the
area will continue to grow.[2]

The other districts of the province can be associated with resource towns. Port Alberni and Campbell River on Vancouver Island, Prince George, Kitimat, Dawson Creek and Cranbrook are all different from each other and associated with different combinations of resources, but all are versions of the mine, mill and rail towns familiar across midnorthern Canada. The aboriginal settlements—Haida, Kwakiutl and Bella Coola, among others—provide a sharp contrast.

British Columbia is a rich and favoured community. Its resource wealth and climate ensure that its status as one of Canada's richest provinces will endure, though the danger of earthquakes associated with the geologic faults along the Pacific shore must always be kept in mind.[3]

II

VISITORS MIGHT BE STRUCK by the seemingly deep ideological disputes in British Columbia politics. Certainly, the vitriol of press comment is unmatched elsewhere in Canada, including Quebec.

The contest between champions of socialist and capitalist views has been going on for more than a century. The province has had a strong union movement and socialist and social democratic political parties, as well as parties of the economic establishment for all this time. Though one might be tempted to say that the bitter debate contributes more to the personal fortunes of political leaders and commentators than to practical policy differences, I am not persuaded by such cynicism.

The debates may differ in subject as the years go by. And the market may become more entrenched in our everyday lives with each passing year. But the gap between a people's approach to public policy, which places primary emphasis on community and family and class, and an approach designed to smooth the path and encourage the profits of corporations in the belief that this alone will ensure the wider community's prosperity seems as wide as ever.

An industrial relations dispute can illustrate the British Columbia context. Fletcher Challenge, a giant lumber-and-paper company, is owned by its New Zealand parent (fifty-one percent) and by shareholders. It operated three pulp-and-paper mills in B.C. which had been shut down by the longest strike in the industry's history —nine months—when workers voted fifty-nine percent in favour of a new contract in April 1998. The 2,400 workers, who earned $50,000 annually on average, had fought off company demands for concessions in 1992 and 1994–95 with strikes of thirty-three and forty-seven days. Their two main unions had targeted Fletcher for the 1997–98 confrontation. They believed that the agreement they signed would set the pattern in the entire B.C. industry.

Yet, seven months into the strike, and just before the negotiations that tipped the scale in favour of approval, the workers voted ninety-three percent against a mediator's report and its proposed settlement. Greg Jones, one of those on strike, said he remained firm in his resolve to resist the company's demands, despite the drastic cut in income his family had sustained: "I became a pipefitter for security for myself and my family and now the company is threatening that security with its demand for flexibility."

The workers were determined to resist "workplace flexibility" as defined by the company. The meaning of this phrase was at the centre of negotiations. If the company view prevailed, management would be able to assign workers to multiple tasks without reference to certain trade jurisdictions. It would also be able to run the mills year-round and through statutory holidays (including the customary Christmas shutdown), and to operate within a six-year contract, much longer than previous deals. Similar arrangements had been struck in eastern North America, according to Fletcher executives, and they believed that they must be free to match the global competition.

The union leaders replied that they and their local union members would like to increase the number of jobs by limiting overtime and perhaps cutting working hours. They regarded the length of the contract as yet another management tactic to undermine the militancy of the union. They feared that the loss of frequent negotiations on issues that mattered, such as wages, hours, the work calendar and the integrity of the trade would distance the workforce from the union itself. These six-, ten- and fifteen-year deals now being presented at the bargaining table might reduce workers' commitment to the principle of worker solidarity.

While the 1997–98 strike continued, Fletcher Challenge actually satisfied its shareholders and met its net income targets. It sold off the large inventory it had been stockpiling for many months, and divested itself of a specialized paper company (for nearly $1 billion, or $300 million after tax) and of a stake in timber lands ($135 million after tax). It cancelled a planned investment in a $220 million

electric-power plant that would have served several Vancouver
Island communities. Some observers called the latter decision a
"capital strike" and interpreted it as an attempt to mobilize community pressure against the workers to push them back to the bargaining table. The company also reduced its debt and restructured (that
is, downsized) its management. As a result, the price of Fletcher
Challenge shares remained firm. Said a market analyst: "Forget
about corporate earnings. . . . The share price tells the story. If you
stand back and look at the results, all that really counts to shareholders is where the share price goes."

The story encapsulates the difference in values between workers and owners. The workers were determined to resist what they
saw as a local institutional expression of "the insatiable demands of
global capital." If workers in eastern Canada and the United States
were prepared to give in on flexible work rules, that was their business. But such a system would not be coming to their communities:
"B.C. is different," said one of their leaders. They waged the struggle in order to maintain a certain degree of stability in the hours
they could dedicate to family life. They saw the negotiation as an
opportunity to increase the number of new jobs available to the next
generation of workers. And they hoped to win security for their
trades in the longer term.

Managers looked at the B.C. mills and the strike in terms of
future profit levels and worldwide competition. President Douglas
Whitehead of Fletcher Challenge Canada said: "We didn't go into
this [strike] lightly. We gave it an awful lot of thought. We have
$2 billion invested here and if we are to get an acceptable return, we
have to do a number of things. Getting world-competitive labour
practices is one of a half-dozen things we have to do." And as long
as the stockholders remained confident in the path he had chosen,
the share would hold its value and the impact on local workers and
communities could be regarded as acceptable. This is the modern
face of class warfare. As it was a century ago, so today it is plainly visible in British Columbia.[4]

III

THE SINGLE MOST PRESSING matter on British Columbia's public
agenda today is a problem in First Nations–government relations.
Most of the aboriginal peoples of British Columbia have never
signed treaties. Thus, unlike most of the rest of Canada, there has

never been a formal recognition of the transfer of sovereignty from aboriginal to French or British or Canadian possession.

Political leaders of the settler society and the courts in British Columbia have maintained that a declaration of sovereignty by the British in the mid-nineteenth century was sufficient to entrench the new order and to extinguish aboriginal claims. But these decisions were taken in an atmosphere (the early Victorian era) that disparaged aboriginal culture and dismissed aboriginal political arguments while assuming that British (and European) culture represented the greatest achievements and the only appropriate index of human endeavour.

A lot has changed in the intervening century. The countries of Europe have themselves been the cause of unprecedented human suffering; the cultures of the traditional peoples have been shown to possess a wisdom that had previously been ignored by outsiders. Thus, the gauges of cultural virtue have changed position.

The shifting balance of these judgments was brought home to Canadians in 1973. Having steadfastly maintained for a century that they must be dealt with as a people, the Nisga'a won a foothold in Canadian law when, in the Calder case, six judges (a majority) of Canada's Supreme Court ruled that aboriginal rights had once existed in British Columbia and three (a minority) also ruled that such rights continued to exist. For the past twenty-five years, British Columbians and Canadians have been struggling to find appropriate political solutions to these dramatic shifts in cultural and legal perception.

Delgamuukw (pronounced del/ga/mook) now occupies the centre of this story in British Columbia. He was a hereditary chief of the Gitxsan in whose name a land claim was launched in 1984. The long civil trial culminated in the dismissal of the case by Chief Justice McEachern of the B.C. Supreme Court in 1991. In his judgment of nearly four hundred pages, the judge ruled that aboriginal rights and land claims had been extinguished by British acts and ordinances before B.C. became a province in 1871.

This decision was largely supported by the B.C. Court of Appeal in its decision of 1993. These judges agreed with McEachern: the First Nations did not possess ownership rights or the right to self-government. However, the Appeal Court judges did find a limited sphere of "Aboriginal rights" that would permit aboriginal people to engage in traditional activities for sustenance and ceremonial purposes. These could be described as "user" rights, not ownership rights, and would apply to personal or community consumption of the fruits of fishing, trapping, hunting and the like. These judges, like McEachern, were following the path set out by B.C. lawmakers and members of the bench during the preceding century.

When the appeal of the Delgamuukw case reached Canada's Supreme Court, however, the country's highest legal body ruled that Mr. Justice McEachern's findings of fact were defective. Fifteen years after the case began, they ordered a new trial. That is where the story stands today.

Why the reversal of McEachern's judgment? What had changed? The justices on the Supreme Court, like scholars around the world and, increasingly, the surrounding popular culture, were giving credence to the memories and stories and folk tales and genealogies that had been passed down by aboriginal people. This willingness to consider oral testimony as having an authority in court equal to that of written documents drastically revised the information available to the court. Jurists who relied on the written word as the sole authority now had to confront the possibility—nay, the Supreme Court's conclusion—that oral traditions must be placed on an "equal footing" with other kinds of historical evidence.[5]

In this landmark ruling, the Supreme Court of Canada provided some important principles to be applied in cases concerning aboriginal title. The most striking aspect of the decision was the statement that aboriginal title was not only a user right, as had once been the view, but rather, constituted a right to exclusive use and occupation. This property right, wrote Chief Justice Antonio Lamer, was not identical to absolute (fee simple) ownership because the lands must be held collectively and could be sold only to the Crown. (These provisions were originally set out in the Royal Proclamation of 1763.) Nevertheless, it was much closer to absolute ownership than had formerly been understood, because it recognized the right of aboriginal people to decide on the use of such lands and also to prevent others from using the land without their consent. The right was limited, Lamer wrote, only in that the lands could not be used in a manner that was "irreconcilable with the nature of the attachment to the land which forms the basis of the group's claim to aboriginal title."[6]

Canada's highest court also set out four tests of aboriginal title. To establish successfully a claim to land, a band must be able to prove:

1. that it occupied the land before the date of British sovereignty (usually understood to be 1846 in British Columbia);
2. that its presence amounted to occupation;
3. that it maintained (though this is a qualified requirement) continuity of occupation; and,
4. that it enjoyed exclusivity of occupation (also a qualified requirement) when the Crown assumed sovereignty.[7]

Each of these tests is grounded solidly in common law and is thus subject to clear methods of debate and resolution. However, the court also declared that the aboriginal perspective must be considered in discovering the facts in any particular case. This is where oral evidence and a nuanced understanding of aboriginal history comes in. It is also where Judge McEachern's conclusions were overruled.

More than ninety percent of British Columbia is Crown land at the present time. Much of this territory is covered by Crown licences for forestry, mining, grazing and rights of way. Now combined aboriginal claims for the recovery of traditional lands cover more than a hundred percent of the province.

What is more, under the British North America Act of 1867, which became part of the 1982 Constitution Act, the federal government is responsible for "lands reserved for Indians." The Supreme Court has said that this phrase must include aboriginal title lands. Thus, federal power to legislate on behalf of aboriginal people now projects into the exclusively provincial powers over lands and property (Section 92 of the same acts). These are matters of central public importance because they affect provincial law and are thrown into the complicated sphere of federal–provincial relations.[8]

The Delgamuukw case will lead either to renewed negotiations between aboriginal communities and the governments of Canada and British Columbia or to further litigation—or both. In the meantime, it has exacerbated racial tensions in public debate.

The British Columbia government's policy during the 1990s has been to negotiate treaties. Unusual in themselves (provinces don't normally negotiate treaties as a matter of course), the discussions have involved the First Nations, the federal government and representatives of the province. Again the heightened profile of the province (compared to Ottawa) in public affairs is evident. The negotiations,

which began under the governments of William Vander Zalm and
Mike Harcourt and have been continued by Premier Glen Clark,
bore fruit in 1998 with the completion of the first British Columbia
treaty of modern times, the Nisga'a settlement reached by the parties
in July 1998.

The issues addressed in the Nisga'a treaty were first raised more
than a hundred years ago, when the Nisga'a challenged the government's assumption that it could dispose of tribal lands. As noted earlier, successive provincial governments went ahead, in their "great
potlatch," to do just that. The consequence has been a century of
conflict, as seen from the aboriginal perspective.

The Nisga'a agreement of 1998 is the first deal to address these
outstanding claims in British Columbia. As Premier Clark has said,
it may be a "template" for future negotiations with other aboriginal
groups. In each case the goal will be to recognize the aboriginal
community's existence and sovereignty, and then to extinguish some
portion of their claim to sovereignty in exchange for grants of land,
money and services. In the case of the Nisga'a treaty, the aboriginal
people have agreed to pay Canadian taxes, a new step for them,
while receiving a cash settlement that will be controlled by the
band. These treaty negotiations are fraught with difficulty. Public
concern about aboriginal issues would have arisen, in any case,
given the circumstances of First Nations–Canada relations, but the
danger of excessive public reaction is great because of the sweeping
nature of the case and the uncertainty it generates. Trevor Lautens,
a B.C. journalist, wittingly or unwittingly illustrated the sudden
leap in the level of popular rhetoric in a column published in April
1998, four months after the Supreme Court's Delgamuukw ruling.
"It must be obvious," he wrote, "that aboriginal ownership of all
British Columbia has now been ratified." In a decade, Lautens predicted, "all Greater Vancouver property 'owners' will pay ground
rent to their three ultimate landlords: the Squamish, Musqueam
and Burrard bands." He speculated that by "around 2025 Vancouver, Victoria and British Columbia will no longer bear those names,
for the same reason that Rhodesia has been renamed Zimbabwe.
The shameful colonial past must be, as totally as possible, expunged.
It's started."[10]

Yes, change will be coming; no, such predictions do not make
the necessary debates easier. Yet Lautens characterizes himself as one
who stands on the side of aboriginal people. He wrote in a column
on Canada's national day that, in his ideal world, "My Canadians,

even (or especially) when aware of their greater power in earliest days of contact, could never have looked into the eyes of an Indian child and stripped his people of their lands and dignity."[11] Lautens recognizes that the people of British Columbia will have to travel a long road of education and reflection during the next generation, but he is ambivalent, perhaps because he recognizes that sincerely held loyalties to party and place are being challenged by the treaty negotiations and by the court's rulings on aboriginal title.

The race-based decisions taken by provincial political leaders during a century of denial, decisions that ignored consistent aboriginal statements of claim, have forced this journey on the people. The long delay in facing the music makes the process all the more difficult today.

The discussion between First Nations people and other Canadians will have to focus on the courts and the law, as well as on the history of the peoples concerned, if rational exchange is to occur. Bob Exell, a member of B.C.'s Department of the Attorney General during the 1980s and one who worked on First Nations policy, argues that the new spate of land claims need not be the cause of economic disaster in the province. Rather, he writes, the important issue associated with the Delgamuukw case concerns the quantity of land subject to aboriginal claim. Was it occupied at all? What was the "intensity of occupation"? He concludes that research and negotiation can produce reasonable settlements.[12] Some argue that the past century saw the exercise of wisdom and foresight by jurists and policy-makers and that the present departure initiated by the Supreme Court ruling is folly. This position can lead to challenges to the very institutions on which Canadian society relies for stability and reason. Melvin Smith, also a former B.C. civil servant, has described the Delgamuukw decision as "one of the most audacious acts of judicial engineering in our history." In a speech to the Vancouver Board of Trade, he criticized the Supreme Court's proposed "flimsy tests" for the establishment of aboriginal occupancy:

> The Chief Justice says that these notions have wide
> support in the "critical literature," meaning the
> product of those academics of a certain ideological
> bent who develop these propositions endlessly,
> largely for the benefit of their own kind. Until now,
> no one seriously thought that the highest court of
> the land would accept such notions. Elsewhere, the

Chief Justice refers with approval to the writings of
the Royal Commission on Aboriginal People. With
respect, he might better have spent his time reading again the judgment of one of his predecessors,
Justice Taschereau, who said in an earlier leading
case on aboriginal title that the practice of the
Crown over the years in dealing with Indian claims
did not imply that the Indians had legal title to the
land. Taschereau said that to find otherwise would
mean "that all progress of civilization and development in this country is and always has been at the
mercy of the Indian race. Some of the writers cited
by the appellants, influenced by sentimental and
philanthropic considerations, do not hesitate to go
as far. But legal and constitutional principles are in
direct antagonism with their theories."

Smith was citing Justice Taschereau's ruling in the crucial case of the
nineteenth century, concerning the St. Catherine's Milling and
Lumber Company, delivered in 1886. Both Smith and Taschereau
would prefer to ignore aboriginal evidence of the type that the
Supreme Court has now ruled admissible.

In the meantime, Smith proposes that the federal government
introduce a legislative solution to the Delgamuukw issue. It should
pass a law, he suggests, that permits a province to infringe lawfully
on any aboriginal title and enables aboriginal groups to seek fair
compensation for losses incurred:

We in Canada should embark upon this more
rational approach to dealing with this difficult
problem. The native leadership will resist the
process because they are not used to having their
views overridden. But they must be reminded that
public support for the land claims process is very
much on the wane. We must deal fairly, but it must
be done in a balanced way, and this is a matter for
governments to decide.

Having lost in the courts, Smith is within the law to turn to governments to defend his position. Interestingly, within a few months
of his speech, the Reform Party signalled its willingness to follow his
proposal.[13]

Perhaps inevitably, some observers in the West are already questioning the national place in such debates. The University of Victoria political scientist Terry Morley wrote: "[T]his distant and disdainful Court places the economic prosperity of British Columbia in grave peril. . . . a court in far away Ottawa, with modes of reasoning foreign to British Columbia's sensibilities, has revived our colonial status and made itself and its subordinate judges our effective rulers."[14] Similar sentiments were expressed in the 1870s. They do not promise political or constitutional peace.

IV

THE ECONOMIC BOOM IN British Columbia began in 1986 and proceeded through eleven unbroken years of growth to the end of 1997, when it slowly ground to a halt. During this period, the province was governed by Social Credit administrations and then by the New Democratic Party. The overheated rhetoric of its press wars continued unabated throughout this period, and so did bitter partisanship, but the dominant tone was optimism and the dominant reality was growth. Talk of Pacific Rim prosperity, Hong Kong immigration and unbounded growth dominated the newspapers both in the province and, not surprisingly, across the country.

The province's metropolitan regions grew, prospered and seemingly functioned effectively as places of increasing social amenities. Trevor Boddy, the architectural writer, returned to Vancouver in 1996 after nine years away to discover

> an ongoing urban experiment in dwelling densities and new forms of housing that is now the envy of the continent. City planners and housing developers arrive here from around the world, eager to ogle our uncharacteristic success in forging a liveable, high-density downtown in a very young city. Downtown Vancouver now has more residents per acre than the centres of San Francisco, Toronto, or Montreal, and it is close to overtaking Manhattan as North America's most densely populated large urban area.[15]

This is the positive side of an exciting metropolis.

British Columbia entered a downturn in 1998. Why? The downturn in Asian economies played a large part, but it's hard to get past the usual political rhetoric to discover such underlying problems. Jock Finlayson of the Business Council of British Columbia blamed provincial taxes and red tape. He said that "the policy agenda of the NDP government since it was elected in 1991, over a period of time, has certainly contributed to our economic problems. It's led to a deterioration in our competitive position as a jurisdiction. It has raised the costs of doing business in B.C. compared with other places. It has tremendously increased the complexity of doing business here because there has been a large increase in the amount of regulation and new legislation."

A university observer, Marjorie Griffin Cohen, denied that policies affecting business had changed during the 1990s and, instead, linked the downturn to the international economic context. She also attributed the conservative rhetoric to business's campaign "to exact whatever concessions it can get from the provincial government."[16]

Indeed, tax cuts surfaced quickly when discussion turned to the government's next steps. The social democratic government had raised the top personal income tax rate, a matter that disturbs those who pay it, but may also affect the knowledge industries, which rely on relatively mobile workers. Thus, legislation that affects the business climate is much more than a matter of personal tax. The dean of UBC's business faculty criticized Premier Clark: "He's going around looking for a big capital-investment solution, a smelter or something that will employ lots of people in union jobs and get him political credit. But in the new economy, things are diversified. And mostly non-union."[17]

Thus, discussion of the economy inevitably turns to debate about industrial-relations law, the government approach to education and medical care, and the entire panoply of public policy.

Ideology and partisanship, visceral at times, dominate public conversation in British Columbia. It may be a surprise, even a shock, to outsiders to discover such intensity, but the vigour of the debate is also refreshing because it offers evidence of a people's commitment to their community.

In 1990 the *Vancouver Sun* published a seven-part series by two UBC planning professors, Alan Artibise and Michael Seelig, on development policy in the lower mainland. The thrust of the series was that potentially high growth rates would require appropriate planning responses. Sound reasonable? Well, some participants in the debate have called foul.

The authors were paid $60,000 by the *Sun*. It is alleged that the idea for the series originated in the development industry and in the concern of its leaders that local residents' groups were becoming too strong and too effective in preventing development projects. Though the editor claims that the idea for the series came to him independently, one of the authors, Artibise, confirms the developer initiative. His own motivation, he says, was "a calculated attempt to change an ideology."

What was the implication? According to Katharyne Mitchell, a geography professor who studied the series of articles, "The way the ideas are presented is to make large-scale growth seem inevitable. There is an effort to attain an aura of objectivity, but those who try to pull the discussion in a different direction are made to seem that they are not speaking rationally or dealing with reality." The series appeared a week before a Vancouver civic election in which an anti-development activist was defeated by an incumbent who stood closer to the pro-growth forces in the city.[18] This is the essence of political debate and is not to be decried. Ideas are aired and paths are chosen. All that is asked of the combatants is that they declare their interest.

British Columbia was the locus of frank ideological discussion in 1900 and it remains so at the end of the twentieth century. The vigour of its debates is a sign of community health, not of weakness.

REFERENCES

1. Tom Barrett, "Numbers show prairie exodus to B.C. is a myth" *Vancouver Sun* 18 April 1998, A1.

2. Chris Rose, "Kelowna destined to be B.C.'s third metropolis" *Vancouver Sun* 13 June 1998, B1.

3. J. Lewis Robinson, "British Columbia" in *The Canadian Encyclopedia* (Edmonton: Hurtig 1985) pp. 218–226.

4. The story of the strike comes from a variety of sources: Gordon Hamilton, "Fletcher separates divisions" *Vancouver Sun* 24 October 1996, C1, and "Moves by Fletcher proved the correct path" 13 February 1997, D1; Paul Luke, "Pulp Talks Loom" *Vancouver Province* 11 February 1997, and "Mill towns beaten to a pulp" 5 April 1998; John Schreiner "Fletcher Challenge strike could be long" *Financial Post* 5 August 1997, and "Strikebound Fletcher sells Blandin subsidiary for US$650M" 1 October 1997; editorial, *Financial Post*, "Unions ignore 'big picture' in Fletcher Challenge fight" 31 October 1997; Patricia Lush "Fletcher cancels plan for B.C. plant" *Globe and Mail* 29 October 1997, and "Fletcher unions reject mediators' report" 21 February 1998; Fred Wilson, "B.C. strike pits workers against foreign capital" *Vancouver Sun* 24 July 1997. I would like to thank Winnipeg representatives of the Communications, Energy, and Paperworkers Union (CEP) for making materials on the strike available to me.

5. Kent McNeil and Lori Ann Roness, "Legalizing Oral History: Proving Aboriginal Claims in Canadian Courts" forthcoming, *Journal of the West* (I would like to thank Professor McNeil for permitting me to see this paper in draft form).

6. Kent McNeil, "Defining aboriginal Title in the 90s: Has the Supreme Court Finally Got It Right?" (Toronto: York University, Robarts Centre for Canadian Studies, Twelfth Annual Robarts Lecture 1998).

7. Kent McNeil, "Aboriginal Rights in Canada: From Title to Land to Territorial Sovereignty" *Tulsa Journal of Comparative and International Law* (forthcoming, 1998, volume 5: pp. 253–298).

8. Kent McNeil, "Aboriginal Title and the Division of Powers:

Rethinking Federal and Provincial Jurisdiction" *Saskatchewan Law Review* 61, 2 (1998) pp. 431–465.

9. Robert Matas, "Nisga'a people make history with B.C. pact" *Globe and Mail* 16 July 1998 A4; "A Cause Worth Fighting For" *The Democrat* (NDP, British Columbia) July 1998; Justine Hunter, "Clark to launch mail campaign on Nisga'a treaty" *Vancouver Sun* 18 April 1998; a comparison of the sharply differing viewpoints can be seen in Stephen Hume, "Campbell takes the low road on treaties" *Vancouver Sun* 18 July 1998, G3, and Gordon Gibson, "How about letting the public in on the Nisga'a deal?" and "Oh, that old land claims process? It's history" *Globe and Mail* 21 July and 26 May 1998; Melvin H. Smith, "The Delgamuukw Case: What Does It Mean and What Do We Do Now?" *Public Policy Sources* #10 (Vancouver: Fraser Institute 1998).

10. Trevor Lautens, "Land Claims Talks Are a Disaster in Making" *Vancouver Sun* 4 April 1998, A23.

11. Trevor Lautens, "Mannered, principled Canadians are too few" *Vancouver Sun* 4 July 1998, A23.

12. Bob Exell, "Definition of Indian occupancy will occupy lawyers for years" *Vancouver Sun* 3 April 1998, A23.

13. Editorial, "Reform throws party at court's expense" *Globe and Mail* 11 June 1998, A22.

14. Terry Morley, in *Vancouver Sun* 20 December 1997 A21, cited in Smith, "The Delgamuukw Case."

15. Trevor Boddy, "The Paradise Pushers" *The Georgia Straight* 2–9 April 1998, pp. 15–18.

16. Jim Boothroyd, "Bloom comes off B.C. boom" *Montreal Gazette* 7 March 1998, B3.

17. Miro Cernetig, "B.C.'s boom goes bust" *Globe and Mail* 21 March 1998, A1, 6.

18. Robert Sarti, "Developers behind 'scholarly' articles predicting growth" reprinted from the *Vancouver Sun* in *New City Magazine* 17, 4 (Summer 1997) p. 37.

CHAPTER EIGHT

Alberta

ALBERTA IS ALLEGEDLY THE noisiest province in English-speaking Canada.[1] It's the tempestuous brother or sister who is not going to be hushed, thank you very much. It has money in its pockets and it's going to make its opinions heard. If it loses the money, it's probably your fault. It will get it back, though, and more, and you'll probably want some when that happens. Significantly, it will share its good fortune. It is headstrong but generous, and it does care about others in the family. And remember, it will pipe up, uninvited and unrepresentative though its message may be, so take with a grain of salt its claim to represent the entire West.[2] Indeed, Edmonton residents won't even acknowledge this caricature as their own, insisting that it's just another Calgary myth.

I

ALBERTA IS CANADA'S FOURTH province in area and population. It is the richest and smallest of the big four, not the leader of the poorer seven. Its major cities, Edmonton, the capital in the central north, and Calgary, home of many corporate head offices in the central south, compete determinedly. These two cities also rank as Canada's fifth- and sixth-largest centres, each heading quickly towards one million in population (the census metropolitan areas exceeded nine hundred thousand in 1998). The province shares the spectacular ranges of the Rocky Mountains with British Columbia and, on the mountains' eastern slopes, it has the distinctive foothills.[3]

The southern half of the province, stretching in a wide arc

from Waterton to Red Deer, is Prairie, much like southern
Saskatchewan and Manitoba. This zone is dry, except for some irrigated tracts in the south, and relatively treeless. The central region
is parkland, again like Saskatchewan and Manitoba, with rolling
hills, valleys, lakes, bluffs of trees and rich soils for field agriculture.
The northern half of the province shares with the other Prairie
provinces a vast boreal forest in which great rivers and lakes
predominate and agriculture is sparse. The one exception to this
generalization is the Peace River region, the northernmost grain-
growing area in the world. Beneath the surface of the land lie the
Devonian and Mesozoic period deposits of plant and animal life
that accumulated when the territory alternated between land and
sea and that now constitute the rich coal, oil and gas reserves that
underwrite the province's wealth.

With the exception of the southwest, Alberta shares the climate
of the Prairie provinces—long, cold winters and short, dry summers,
and plenty of sunshine in both seasons. The chinook winds that flow
through the southern Rockies warm the southwest periodically in
winter, making that the more temperate climate. Mean tempera-
tures in January are -8C in the south and -24C in the north, a difference that has to be experienced to be appreciated.[4]

Like British Columbia, Alberta has been growing rapidly for a
decade. The province accounted for about one-fourth of the West's
population between 1921 and 1951, but then started to grow and now
contains about one-third of the total, or nearly three million people.

Calgary is the city of the moment in western Canada. It has
endured tough times in the recent past, but its population grew by
thirty percent in the fifteen years after 1981 and it is now "the fastest-
growing major city in Canada."[5] Like Vancouver, it is a magnet for
the young, who see the recreational potential of nearby mountains
and wilderness zones such as Banff, Canmore and Kananaskis, and
who enjoy the ambiance of a dynamic city. Calgary has the second-
highest concentration of corporate head offices in Canada, after
Toronto (Suncor, CP Rail, Dow Chemical and Shaw Communications among them), and its housing market and traffic problems are
tiny compared to those in Vancouver and Toronto.[6]

Edmonton's population is probably a little older, according to a
demographic breakdown by age, but the capital city possesses many
of the advantages—new housing stock, efficient transportation
infrastructure, good education and health facilities—of its bump-
tious (as Edmontonians would put it) neighbour. It came closer to

losing its prized professional hockey team, but the private sector managed to muster sufficient resources in the nick of time during 1997–98. Edmonton is the government town. Though it often loses the hype wars to its brash sibling, it is a pleasant, midsized (on a world scale) Canadian city with the range of ethnic, class and aboriginal questions that affect all the Prairie centres.

The next tier of cities—Lethbridge, Medicine Hat, Red Deer, Lloydminster, Camrose, Fort McMurray and Grande Prairie—are comfortable, attractive centres of the type familiar throughout western North America. Agriculture and industry sustain them, the Chamber of Commerce and service clubs govern them, sports and special festival events (usually volunteer-driven) preoccupy them. They are consistently European in ethnic stock. Their churches are full on Sundays. They are prone to boosterism, but they are also much more likely to be growing than their counterparts in Saskatchewan and Manitoba. They have all the amenities of North American life, given the limitations of a population of ten to eighty thousand, but not the special characteristics, including overt conflict, of the metropolis.

Like British Columbia, Alberta for the past generation has perpetually been a "have" province, meaning that the increase in the annual provincial gross domestic product (a rough measure of total wealth) exceeded the national average. Despite sharp fluctuations in energy revenue, its wealth has been sufficiently obvious to the rest of the country to invoke regular expressions of envy from citizens living to the east. Even in a momentary downturn in energy prices, as in 1998, this will not change.

II

To CHARACTERIZE THE ALBERTA role on the national stage as the rambunctious sibling will seem unfair to Albertans and probably patronizing. My defence will be resumed in several later chapters but one aspect of my case rests on Albertans' response—and I do mean all Albertans, not just the government—to the economic cycle of 1973–81 (boom) and 1981–87 (recession).[7]

Albertans see themselves as entrepreneurial, and their culture is, indeed, more supportive of economic enterprise and individual productivity than any other in Canada. It seems that every conversation notes at least one "amazing inspirational testimonial" wherein a former gas-field worker or building caretaker begins knitting toques or molding chocolate mints in a disused shed and—boom!—is now worth a million, maybe two. The image sits at the heart of this distinctive culture. The Albertan does not emphasize the delightful and different quality of the province's natural environment, as does the British Columbian, but rather the vigour and competitiveness and the go-it-alone quality of its residents.

Even the austere language of the economist cannot conceal the Alberta enthusiasm for risk. Robert Mansell, chair of the Economics Department at the University of Calgary, has described the society that took shape in the 1970s:

> Alberta . . . had become a modern, largely urban society. The residents had achieved a standard of living and per capita income about equal to the Canadian average. Almost half were born in other provinces or countries and came to the province in search of economic opportunity. This self-selection meant that a high proportion of the population could be classified as risk-takers: entrepreneurial, mobile, and economically motivated. Their values and the overall character of the province had also been profoundly shaped by Alberta's industrial heritage. Both the agriculture and petroleum industries tend to be typified by capital-intensive production processes, a high degree of risk, externally determined and highly variable prices and policies, and a large number of independent producing units. The development of the petroleum sector simply enhanced the basically rural conservative values of rugged individualism, risk-taking, entrepreneurship, and a unique mix of self-reliance and co-operation. . . . there was not a broad base in Alberta for organized labour or the associated values. There was a widespread respect for and acceptance of market forces and the need to adjust to shifts in the market.[8]

A social democrat or environmentalist might have sketched this story quite differently, perhaps as a battle over how fast to sell off Alberta's oil and gas, at what price, and how the revenues were to be distributed among national and provincial governments, energy corporations, consumers and classes of individual workers. But that

would be to apply a national class or ecological analysis to a subject
that Albertans preferred to see as a case of "us against the world,"
and especially against the rest of Canada.

Energy prices shot up in the 1970s, to the advantage of all parties. This made the business of revenue allocation particularly exciting. Having fought between 1870 and 1930 to win local control over
public lands and natural resources (a power taken for granted in all
the other provinces of Canada, but not permitted the Prairie governments before 1930), Prairie Canadians may have sympathized a
little with Albertans in their struggles with Ottawa. Premier Peter
Lougheed ensured that the province received larger revenues during
the 1970s than had been the case in the preceding two decades. The
sharp rise in oil prices, from about $3 a barrel in the early 1970s to
nearly $30 in 1980, made his task easier.

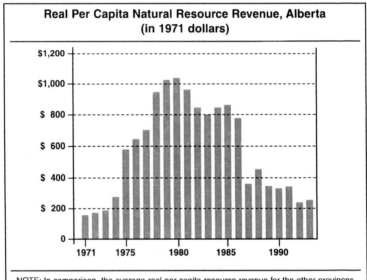

**Real Per Capita Natural Resource Revenue, Alberta
(in 1971 dollars)**

NOTE: In comparison, the average real per capita resource revenue for the other provinces
has typically been less than $50.

SOURCE: Population figures from Cansim matrices 6369-72 and 6219-23. Provincial CPI
indexes from matrices 1860-9. Financial Management Sytem (FMS) data for resource
revenues from matrices 2808-17.

From Robert Mansell "Fiscal Restructuring in Alberta: An Overview" in Christopher Bruce
et al. eds. *A Government Reinvented: A Study of Alberta's Deficit Elimination Program.*
(Toronto: Oxford University Press, 1997) p. 23.

Two forces were at work to make the Alberta condition more
complicated than this would imply. First, "in spite of the historical evidence that periods of rapid growth are typically relatively

short-lived and almost always end in 'bust,'" as Mansell pointed out, "there seems to be great difficulty in containing the psychology of extrapolation." This is an economist's way of saying that people in the middle of a boom expect the boom to go on forever. Second, as both Mansell and Kenneth Norrie have argued, "there is a funda-mental conflict even for governments that recognize a boom and see an increased need to diversify or otherwise to achieve a more stable and sustainable economy ... a booming resource sector will tend to result in an economy even more specialized in, and dependent on, that sector."[9] This is the "staple trap"—once into a boom, support-ers pour all their work into the single activity that pays so well. Alberta has had to struggle to overcome both defects.

Ottawa and the rest of the country, paupers by comparison, tried to elbow their way into Alberta's resource revenue windfall in 1980 by means of the Trudeau government's National Energy Program. This is where the truculence of the Alberta sibling solidified into a life force. As soon as the federal government increased its take of energy royalties, oil corporations retaliated by moving their business out of the province. The consequent economic downturn, much sharper than in the rest of the country, reinforced the Albertan sense of grievance against Ottawa. To make matters worse, in 1984-85, just after the new Mulroney government deregulated domestic oil prices as Albertans had wished, the world oil price dropped by half and grain prices fell sharply, converting a partial recovery into a deeper recession. Alberta's growth rate was below the national average from 1982 to 1988. It might seem excessive to point out, but I can't resist, that even with resource revenues at less than one-third their earlier levels, and despite the lowest taxation levels in the country, the Alberta government's total budgetary revenue (per capita) was still higher than the average revenue (per capita) of all the other provinces.

The bust, or recession, of 1981–87 seared its image into the hearts of Albertans. The only explanation of the crisis that has sur-vived in the public memory is that Ottawa—Pierre Trudeau and his French Canadian allies, notably Energy Minister Marc Lalonde—caused the collapse. It would be fair to say that the turmoil of the 1980s stands out more sharply in the public memory of Albertans than does the Great Depression of the 1930s and, certainly, the "Borden line" that imposed artificially high oil prices on Ontarians during the 1960s. Thus, the Alberta reaction to the National Energy Program will have to be taken into account in any future discussions about revising the Canadian federation.

If the boom is phase one in the development of a distinctive contemporary Alberta culture and the bust is phase two, then the Klein budgets of 1993 and 1994 are phase three. Why should a mere budgetary strategy rank so highly in popular culture? Because it captured the imagination of the province and the country, promised tough visible cuts in government and delivered them in highly contentious, socially painful doses, the likes of which Canadians had never seen, at least not since the Great Depression. According to supporters and opponents alike, it represented a drastic reduction in the role of government.

Premier Klein's "revolution," as it was styled by government press agents, consolidated the self-perception of Albertans as the frontiersmen and -women who dared to live differently and, by taking such risks, who dared to prosper. Is it any wonder they jib when effete outsiders try to take the locals' hard-won dividends?

What did Ralph Klein do? First, in the months after he won the provincial Conservative party leadership and the premier's office in December 1992, he decided to make new adaptations to the reality that Alberta had "one of the least stable regional economies in Canada."[10] He would work within the obvious constraint of the province's reliance on oil and gas revenues, but he would take new policy directions in coping with this uncertain boon.

Second, Klein acknowledged that the attempts of his predecessors, Lougheed and Getty, to diversify the economy, while they probably had some success, would be impossible to defend in an electoral battle. After all, the government had had to write off almost $2.4 billion in investment losses as a result of these intiatives, far more than had occurred in New Democrat Manitoba where the government was chased from office in 1988.[11] Indeed, the closer parallel, the Conservative Devine administration in Saskatchewan, had just been wiped from the map in a general election for comparable sins.

Third, Klein accepted the thesis that the Alberta economy was already undergoing a dramatic restructuring as a result of the Free Trade Agreement and increasing international competitive pressures. These forces were creating a more outward-looking and efficient private sector, this argument said, and the same process—"downsizing, consolidation of assets, reductions in overheads, and streamlining to allow faster adjustment to a rapidly changing market environment"—should be introduced to a sluggish governmental sector.[12]

Fourth, Klein accepted an unpalatable assessment of the provincial government's spending pattern over the previous two decades: Albertans had become accustomed to higher per capita spending and these higher levels were now "deeply entrenched." As Mansell noted,

> Not only had the "expectations benchmark" been raised, but the capital expenditures (especially on such things as hospitals) had put in place a fairly rigid stream of operating cost obligations. In addition ... the traditional budgetary processes made it very difficult to achieve anything more than modest reductions in constant dollar expenditures through keeping expenditure increases below the rate of inflation.[13]

Finally, Klein chose to maintain the low-tax regime that Albertans were said to regard as a birthright and that he could sell as "a key element of competitive advantage" over all other provinces in Canada.[14]

How to introduce the new regime? Klein accepted the advice of the former New Zealand finance minister, Roger Douglas, who in the early 1990s had become an international crusader for smaller government: cut quickly, cut deeply, cut across the board in every aspect of government. In September 1993 the government announced that it would reduce program spending by 21.7 percent in four years, a per capita cut in real terms of twenty-seven percent. There are two ways to see the Klein action:

1. Facing the fastest-growing debt in the country and a substantial deficit that would resist lesser measures, Klein had to cut spending or raise taxes. He chose one tough course over another.

2. Facing a net debt still very small in relation to the size of the provincial economy (compared to that of the other provinces and of Ottawa), with per capita revenues still above the average of the other provinces and with the lowest tax regime in the country (no provincial sales tax and personal income tax rates at 45.5 percent of the federal rate versus 50–69 percent in other provinces), Klein seized the opportunity to

implement an ideologically driven program that
reduced the size and scope of government to the
advantage of market-based entrepreneurs.

Both explanations are correct. Klein saw a popular strategy,
stole a potential Opposition platform, addressed a small budgeting
dilemma and appealed to two populist emotions in Alberta—the
frontier preference for small government and the entrepreneurial
delight in low taxes.[15]

III

IT IS TOO EASY to say that Alberta is a one-song choir and to suggest, as I have been doing, that one image—the tempestuous spoiled
child of Confederation—can capture its political and social reality.
In truth, the debates in Alberta are as polarized as elsewhere in
the country. The difference lies in the distinctive political culture
within which all Albertans operate.

The 1986 election of Don Getty as successor to Peter
Lougheed was a somewhat reluctant act, accompanied as it was by
the victory of twenty-two Opposition members, including sixteen
New Democrats and four Liberals. Only forty-seven percent of
voters turned out, compared to sixty-six percent in 1982. Still, the
Conservatives received fifty-one percent of the popular vote (sixty-
two percent in 1982), compared to twenty-nine percent for the NDP
and twelve percent for the Liberals.

Getty maintained his seat margin in the 1989 election, but saw
his share of the popular vote slip to forty-four percent compared
with twenty-six percent for the NDP and twenty-nine percent for the
Liberals. (The Conservatives won fifty-nine seats, the NDP sixteen,
and the Liberals eight). The turnout was slightly higher, fifty-four
percent.

The campaign of 1993, Klein's first as leader, was a close-run
contest. An effective Liberal leader and a weaker NDP produced an
important swing in popular vote within the Opposition. Klein won
44.5 percent of the vote, the Liberals 39.7 percent, and the NDP
11 percent. This was far from an electoral sweep and, indeed, was
similar to the proportion of votes allocated to the winner in many
three-sided provincial contests in recent decades. Alberta was not a
one-party state and Klein was not an unchallenged emperor.[16]

The divisions in Alberta politics and society fall in the predictable
places. How to deal with the uncertainty of a small, resource-rich,

energy-exporting economy ranks high on every citizen's list of political questions. The environmental implications of resource development also cause concern. How to cope with rapid growth, especially in urban areas, is a thorny problem, made worse by the great gap between the social experience of rural and small-town Alberta and that of the metropolises. And the issue of wealth distribution—the gulf between the very rich and the very poor—bedevils Alberta, too.

The price of oil dropped like a stone in 1998. After a banner year in 1997 when the provincial economy grew by 6.5 percent (compared to the national average of 3.8 percent and to rates of less than two percent in Atlantic Canada), the expectations for 1998 had to be revised downward. Interestingly, since the oil price was returning to levels set in 1986, the cautious response within the province could be seen as the voice of hard-earned experience, of veterans who had endured the collapse of the 1980s, who hoped that the subsequent diversification would shield the province at least a little, and who were determined to live with the inevitable swings in their fortunes.[17]

The broader question concerned the long-term implications of Alberta's reliance on American markets. Only a detailed map of oil and gas pipelines on the continent, scaled to illustrate the construction of lines south from Alberta and B.C. in the previous decade, could illustrate the change in the energy economy. Mel Hurtig, the well-known Edmonton-based nationalist, argues: "What we're doing—almost blindly—is leaving ourselves in a position where we're going to be extraordinarily vulnerable to OPEC in the future and to interruptions of supply from possible wars."

The principle of Canadian energy self-sufficiency, which moved the Trudeau administrations of the 1970s and early 1980s, has been abandoned by both its Conservative and Liberal successors. Alberta, which is said to have lost $68 billion on differential pricing alone in the 1973–85 period, is the big winner. A second group to gain is the American consumer. As oil industry analyst Ian Doig has commented, "The United States customers should be very thankful for the benevolence of Canadian taxpayers."

The Canadian people have accepted this new policy direction and government assurances about future supplies. Federal Energy Minister Anne McLellan, herself an Albertan, said in 1995: "We are a government committed to market forces determining outcomes. One of my intense aggravations is that people treat the

resource sectors as so-called sunset industries and not part of the
new economy. There are more reserves under the ground in northern Alberta than in Saudi Arabia."

Environmental activists are not convinced. Said one: "For a cold
country like Canada to be so blithely getting rid of its fossil-fuel
resources is just nuts." But the opponents of exports have not won
much attention during the 1990s. In the meantime, the rate of gas
exports to the United States continues to climb exponentially, and
corporations are lining up to ship more gas into the rich Chicago
market.[18]

The environmental challenge affects not only energy developments in Alberta but also its mining and forestry. Several conservation campaigns of the kind familiar to British Columbia
have emerged in recent years, and a unique wrinkle has affected
federal–provincial discussions about the development plans in
national parks, which are located in the province but regulated by
Ottawa. Critics question the health implications of some of the oil
and gas wells, and particularly of "sour gas." Another environmental issue, as in B.C., turns on the revenue potential of tourism. A
recent study of the Yellowstone to Yukon wilderness corridor has
argued that ninety-seven percent of the growth in personal income
in the United States portion of this zone between 1972 and 1997
originated in "industries not connected with the extraction of natural resources," and makes similar claims for Canada.[19] Such issues
must, almost inevitably, remain on the public agenda.

The rates of growth in the province, especially in the two big
cities, cause significant disruptions, too. Hospitals in Edmonton,
schools in Calgary, rapid transit, and zoning and development plans
can all become hot issues because of the need to reconfigure expensive services as quickly as possible. The gulf between city and country, and the urban demand for provincial funding, make such
matters politically sensitive. Two Calgary-based observers, David
Bercuson and Barry Cooper, write of their city:

> The problems are not hard to list. Although there
> are plans for new LRT services, roads, green belts
> and even bike paths and river walks, there is pre-
> cious little money for any of them. There are still
> five police districts instead of the six planned.
> There is a massive transfer from the wallets of Cal-
> garians to the tax coffers. . . .

Those who work in the "high-rise core," the "business and community leaders who know the city's energy sector runs on
natural gas, not oil, and who believe the [provincial] government's
parsimoniousness has gone too far," must confront another
camp—the "rural MLAS" who do not want to loosen the purse
strings.[20]

The rural fiscal conservatives and the urban progressive conservatives have been able to make common cause in the Lougheed,
Getty and Klein Conservative party until now. They have also found
a home in the federal Reform Party. The foundation of the alliance
is the distinctive entrepreneurial culture of Alberta. As Reform MP
Diane Ablonczy said, extending the Alberta myth to encompass all
of western Canada (a habitual imperial gesture in the Reform
Party), "[in] the West there is a can-do attitude. Instead of seeking
help from government, it's 'get the government out of my face, I'll
look after things.' It's an important dynamic in Canada and ensures
government does only what it should be doing."[21] This view can be
found all over the world, not just in western Canada. But it has
become the foundation of a distinctive Alberta outlook. It encoun-
ters serious challenges when rapid development and an apparent
need for such services as roads and health care encounter anti-
government sentiments. Bercuson and Cooper forecast a rift in
Alberta Conservative ranks over just this issue. In any case, the existence of the debates suggests that, despite the consecutive defeats of
more liberal parties, there remains a competitive political environment—not at all a one-note choir—in Alberta today.

REFERENCES

1. I would like to thank Kenneth Norrie and E. J. Chambers of the University of Alberta, Robert Mansell and Herbert Emery of the University of Calgary, and the curatorial staff of the Alberta Provincial Museum for conversations on Alberta and the western Canadian economy.

2. For an illustration of the interpretation that the economic downturn of the 1980s was the fault of outsiders, see "Albertans blame NEP for their economic woes" *Globe and Mail*, 2 June 1987, B6.

3. The population estimates appeared in Jim Cunningham, "Calgary population set to pass Edmonton" *Vancouver Sun* 1 August 1998, B1, 3. The most extensive recent history of Alberta is by Howard Palmer with Tamara Palmer, *Alberta: A New History* (Edmonton: Hurtig 1990).

4. The irrigated zone covers 162,000 hectares. Robert M. Stamp, "Alberta" in *The Canadian Encyclopedia* (Edmonton: Hurtig 1985) pp. 35–42.

5. Alanna Mitchell, "Calgary growing by leaps and bounds" *Globe and Mail* 15 July 1998, A4.

6. Brian Laghi, "Calgary reaps a renaissance" *Globe and Mail* 3 January 1996, A1; to be fair, note that Calgary had 90 head offices to Toronto's 118, but that Toronto suburbs accounted for more than a hundred additional head offices. Montreal had 89, Vancouver 49 and Winnipeg 19, according to this June 1995 count by the Calgary Economic Development Authority.

7. An interesting view of the era is the National Film Board's "Riding the Tornado," a 1987 film written and directed by Bob Lower.

8. Robert Mansell, "Fiscal Restructuring in Alberta: An Overview" in Christopher Bruce, Ronald Kneebone and Kenneth McKenzie, eds., *A Government Reinvented: A Study of Alberta's Deficit Elimination Program* (Toronto: Oxford University Press 1997) pp. 21–2.

9. Mansell, "Fiscal Restructuring in Alberta" pp. 26, 27.

10. Mansell, "Fiscal Restructuring in Alberta" p. 33.

11. According to the Alberta Taxpayers Association, the top ten losers included government write-offs on NovAtel ($646M), Swan Hills Waste Treatment ($410M), Lloydminster Bi-Provincial Upgrader ($392M), Gainers Foods ($209M), Millar Western ($199M), Magnesium Company of Canada ($164M), Syncrude ($81M), Chembiomed ($58M), Northern Lite Canola ($51M) and General Systems Research ($31M).

12. Mansell, "Fiscal Restructuring in Alberta" p. 34.

13. Mansell, "Fiscal Restructuring in Alberta" p. 39.

14. Mansell, "Fiscal Restructuring in Alberta" p. 46.

15. The importance of the Klein budget policy is attested by the appearance of three noteworthy books on it: Kevin Taft, *Shredding the Public Interest* (Edmonton: University of Alberta 1997); Trevor Harrison and Gordon Laxer, eds., *The Trojan Horse: Alberta and the Future of Canada* (Montreal: Black Rose 1995); Christopher J. Bruce, Ronald D. Kneebone, Kenneth J. McKenzie, eds, *A Government Reinvented: A Study of Alberta's Deficit Elimination Program* (Toronto: Oxford University Press 1997). Note also Jim Dinning's defence of the government path. He was the treasurer in the Klein government during this period. His essay "Why we had to cut spending" (*Globe and Mail* 24 March 1997, A19) concludes that only spending cuts or tax increases would eliminate the deficit.

16. The same pattern held true, roughly, in the March 1997 election. The results are discussed in Keith Archer, "Voting Behaviour and Political Dominance in Alberta, 1971–1991" and in Alan Tupper and Roger Gibbins, eds., *Government and Politics in Alberta* (Edmonton: University of Alberta Press 1992). The mid-1980s are surveyed in Andrew Nikiforuk, Sheila Pratt, Don Wanagas, *Running on Empty: Alberta after the Boom* (Edmonton: Newest Press 1987).

17. Bruce Little, "Alberta leads the way in hot economy" *Globe and Mail* 15 May 1998, B9; Mathew Ingram, "Oil patch screws tighten" *Globe and Mail* 29 June 1998, B2; Brent Jang, "Alberta backpedals on oil production" *Globe and Mail* 14 July 1998, A3; Stephen Ewart, "Oil falls to 11.56US; no panic in patch" *Calgary Herald* 16 June 1998, A1.

18. The above discussion of oil draws on Brent Jang, "Oil patch looks south" *Globe and Mail* 9 December 1995, B1; recent developments in natural gas are discussed in articles by Mathew Ingram, "Too much gas, or not enough," "Alberta is a gas, gas, gas" and "Oil patch screws tighten" *Globe and Mail* 2 March, 6 April, 29 June 1998.

19. Alanna Mitchell, "Lifestyles of wild, woodsy key to Rockies' economy" *Globe and Mail* 22 April 1998, A3; the report, by Ray Rasker, released by the Washington-based Wilderness Society, was entitled, "The New Challenge: People, Commerce and the Environment in the Yellowstone to Yukon Region." Other discussions are noted in Alanna Mitchell, "Rare Rockies wilderness at risk: Environmental panel says Alberta's Whaleback should be drilled, mined, logged" and "Alberta activists jubilant over court ruling on environment" *Globe and Mail* 20 May, 11 July 1998; also Andrew Nikiforuk, "Taking the axe to Alberta's forests" *Globe and Mail* 22 June 1998, A1.

20. David Bercuson, Barry Cooper, "The coming rift among Alberta's Conservatives" *Globe and Mail* 18 July 1998, D2; illustrations of other issues include Brian Laghi, "Edmonton hospitals cancel most elective surgery" and Tom Flanagan, "If this school neglects you, try that one" *Globe and Mail* 27 February and 16 July 1998 respectively.

21. Peter O'Neil, "Reform MP rejects traditional stereotype" *Vancouver Sun* 18 July 1998, B4.

CHAPTER NINE

Saskatchewan

SASKATCHEWAN HAS SEEN ITS fortunes rise and fall several times during the twentieth century. For much of its history it has been dominated by agriculture. Yet it is more urban than rural today, by a margin of nearly two to one.[1] It is the home of intensely, famously, partisan politics. It is also the source of co-operative solutions to public policy questions, such as the first state-run hospital insurance and medical insurance in Canada, the first state-run automobile insurance, the first provincially owned bus-transportation company and, recently, a new venture in co-operatives launched when the giant agricultural co-op, the Saskatchewan Wheat Pool, sold shares in a public offering on the Toronto Stock Exchange. It also saw the privatization of several large, publicly owned corporations during the 1980s. Today, it faces great challenges in social and economic affairs.

I

SASKATCHEWAN IS THE ARCHETYPAL Prairie province. The southern half is flat, though the landscape is sufficiently rolling and contains enough striking hills and valleys that local residents are entitled to object when outsiders describe it as boring. Water is an issue of central public importance in southern Saskatchewan. Always in a moisture deficit, the agricultural zones rely upon precipitation and river flows, the latter from snow melt in the Rockies, both of which vary tremendously from year to year.

Only half the province is agricultural. The other half is pre-Cambrian shield, the rocks and lakes and trees of the pre-Cambrian formation so familiar to eastern Canada. Here are the hard-rock mines, the fishing, the hunting, the trapping and the logging of the traditional primary economy.

Saskatchewan's economy actually conforms to the stereotype that outsiders apply to all the western provinces. Its major exports are the products of farms, on the one hand, and of resource extraction—oil and potash and uranium—on the other. Half of the goods shipped out of the country travel south to the United States. Its wheat fields do extend from horizon to horizon, at least in the southern parts of the province.

The society, too, will seem familiar by reputation, if not from personal experience. Its population is aging. The total population has changed very little during the past thirty years and now numbers just over one million. This constitutes about ten percent of the West's population, whereas at the peak of the province's influence in Canada, during the interwar years, it numbered nearly 900,000, about one-quarter of the entire western community. The fastest-growing segment of society is aboriginal. And, in the two larger cities, there are small communities of South Asian, Vietnamese, Filipino and Chinese origin. About half the families in the province can trace a branch to the British Isles, and most of the rest to other European nations.

Saskatoon is the largest city in the province. At 220,000, it is modest in size but often described as one of the most attractive cities in the country. The banks of the South Saskatchewan River form a continuous chain of green space and recreational venues through the city's heart. The University of Saskatchewan, founded in 1907, a campus made harmonious by its limestone-clad buildings, dominates the river's higher east bank. Gardens surrounding a chateau-style railway hotel, an art gallery and a Native Canadian cultural centre stretch along the west bank. And seven bridges span the ribbon of water—or ice—linking the community in a functional and attractive manner.

Regina, the provincial capital, is only slightly smaller in population, about 200,000, and sits in a vast flat plain of wheat fields. It is, appropriately, the headquarters of the world's largest grain-handling co-operative, the aforementioned Saskatchewan Wheat Pool and, since the late nineteenth century, of the training facilities for the Royal Canadian Mounted Police and its predecessor, the North-West Mounted Police. At the city's heart lies Wascana Lake, an artificial creation that stretches several miles from the Legislature, provincial museum and arts centre to the University of Regina. One of the city's prized possessions is a football team, the Saskatchewan Roughriders. Like Saskatoon, with which it is often compared, sometimes unfavourably, Regina offers a pleasant face in summer and a somewhat more austere countenance in January.

The smaller cities of Saskatchewan—Moose Jaw, Prince Albert (both under 40,000 population), North Battleford, Yorkton and Swift Current (under 20,000)—are district service centres for the farms and villages and First Nations reserves that dot the southern half of the province. As in the rest of the West, these cities have local colleges and university extension courses, and its citizens are active in such sports as curling and golf.

Saskatchewan is built on agriculture and the exploitation of natural resources. Its strength for much of this century, and at present, is its ability to adapt to changing international realities. It is a province that takes its politics seriously.

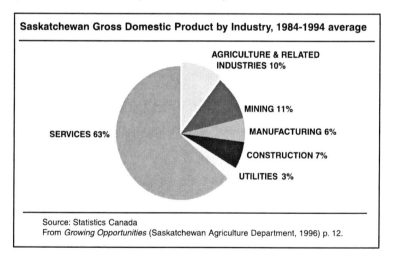

Saskatchewan Gross Domestic Product by Industry, 1984-1994 average

AGRICULTURE & RELATED INDUSTRIES 10%

MINING 11%

MANUFACTURING 6%

CONSTRUCTION 7%

UTILITIES 3%

SERVICES 63%

Source: Statistics Canada
From *Growing Opportunities* (Saskatchewan Agriculture Department, 1996) p. 12.

11

THE PROVINCE REMAINS DEPENDENT on farms. Nearly half of its international merchandise exports are drawn from farms—cereals, oil seeds, vegetable and animal products—and the total, nearly $4.5 billion, illustrates the community's heavy reliance on these workers. One-quarter of these goods travel south to the United States, three-quarters to the rest of the world.

Newcomers may be surprised to hear so many reports of droughts or hailstorms on daily newscasts in summer, but these topics are justifiable preoccupations of the public. In Saskatchewan, where almost every urban household is linked through family to farms, and where the larger economy is so dependent on farm fortunes, such matters as the weather affect everyone. Similarly, the rapid depopulation of rural areas and the extraordinary changes in rural society in the past few decades have caused considerable anxiety in the province.

Value-added production, diversification and market-based signals of price and cost have become the new mantras of Saskatchewan agricultural policy. The new immigration brochures, a revival of the turn-of-the-century literature that attracted the first generation of European families to these plains, still speak of the "vigour" of the climate, emphasize the work ethic of the society and insist that the family farm is "both a business and a way of life." But the brochures now make the case that Saskatchewan fields are "among the least contaminated" in the world. The government's role in the rural community is said to be not income support, but rather, "assisting in the structural adjustments of the sector." The adoption of plant and animal seed stock from around the world, such as Charolais and Simmental beef cattle, is also emphasized. And, too, "it is just a matter of time" before food processing is a major aspect of the local economy. This is a new farm economy, the Saskatchewan brochures say, and if you would like to be part of a forward-looking industry in attractive, opportunity-filled surroundings, consider emigrating.[2]

This *is* a new agricultural economy, one that developed between the 1970s and the 1990s. It probably started with the debates over the marketing of canola (once known as rapeseed) and the transportation system. The key step, however, was the 1993 trade deal within the General Agreement on Tariffs and Trade. This international trade negotiation resolved to set limits on the use of export subsidies. Unquestionably the Crow freight rate was such a subsidy. In order to secure greater access to foreign markets, in other words, Canadian negotiators gave up the Prairie farmers' historic transportation deal. The actual demise of the Crow was announced in 1995, when the federal government said it would provide payouts to farmers to compensate them, once and for all, for the loss of this historic advantage.[3]

Why the transition? The Thatcher and Reagan administrations, which effected great changes in perceptions of government and trade during the 1980s, constitute part of the answer. A shorter-term analysis would note the determination of the Chrétien government in Canada to cut budget deficits and travel rapidly down the path of freer trade and greater economic diversification based on market signals. And in the late 1990s, sharp fluctuations in the price of farm commodities have put great pressure on every rural business.

Innovation Place, a research-and-development park located next to the university campus in Saskatoon, is the Saskatchewan showcase for the agricultural transition. The laboratories in this pleasant setting are supposed to lead a provincial drive to become the Canadian home for agricultural biotechnology, the third of the sectors, alongside health and the environment, in the trio of biotechnologies. A government-sponsored committee on the development of the sector has reported that one-third of the country's biotech firms (thirty companies and four hundred employees, producing $42 million in sales in 1995) are located in Saskatchewan.

The Protein Oil and Starch Pilot Plant Corporation, founded in 1977 to investigate new technologies associated with canola oil, represents the new world of agriculture. It moved into the study of food processing in the 1980s and eventually added projects on cosmetic ingredients.[4] In this and other similar ventures, the provincial government has encouraged basic research and development on the grounds that the federal authorities are backing away from such long-term commitments. The university has tried to get away from the "publish or perish" approach to science and instead is starting to accept the necessity of marketing its technological breakthroughs. A provincial committee on biotechnology has proposed that the government aid the university to overcome the "poor perception" of the province based on "climate and location," by offering job security and higher salaries to promising researchers.[5] This, too, is the new agriculture.

The shift from the Crow rate to market costs in farm transportation, which increased the local availability of cheap animal feed, has also increased interest in animal husbandry, notably hogs. The vast "empty" spaces of rural Saskatchewan are advertised as ideally suited to such enterprises.[6] As a result, the provincial government has encouraged large-scale hog production, recruited farmers in western Europe and engaged in a year-long debate over its provincially run hog-marketing agency. The monopoly agency closed in 1998, replaced by a private sector marketing company that has signed most hog producers, representing about eighty-five percent of the crop, to delivery contracts.[7] However, the collapse of hog prices in 1998 has also left many farm families wondering whether they can survive their entrepreneurial gamble.

Such changes in agriculture place great stress on the provincial transportation system, which formerly relied on a vast elevator and railway network to carry grain to export terminals. Saskatchewan brags that it has twice the roads per capita of any other Canadian province but now admits, too, that the road beds must be reinforced to carry the increasingly heavy traffic. Farmers spend more time in their trucks, too, a result of reduced rail mileage and sharply reduced numbers of elevators, the latter dropping from 900 in 1972 to perhaps 100 by 2004. Increased animal production, much of which travels to the United States by truck, also puts additional pressure on the roads. The government reports that truck crossings at the border increased from 200 to 465 per day between 1988 and 1994. Once again, we encounter an expression of the growing regionalization of the continental economy.[8]

The economy grows, exports increase and the province can sustain more services. But does the individual farm family gain by all this change? Its members learn to compete in a new environment and to become responsible for a wider range of economic decisions. Is this a gain? One such farmer, speaking for a group of his neighbours near Shaunavon, Saskatchewan, replied: "I can't see any benefits to us. Farmers lose. Communities lose. I guess the one benefit I got out of it was to realize I can't trust or depend on government. It was a good lesson."

His conclusion is, in part, cynical and misleading. Canadians, through their government's policy decisions, have chosen to enter the market more wholeheartedly than they had done in the preceding sixty years. This choice entailed less reliance on government. It also disrupted Prairie agricultural communities and Prairie farm families. This is not a case in which one's trust in government has been betrayed: the Chrétien government did exactly what it had promised and what had been coming under its predecessor, the Mulroney Conservatives. Rather, the economic and social transition illustrates how important government policy and decisions can be.

But this farmer is also right: he can no longer rely on government to cushion his dealings with the marketplace to the extent that his parents and grandparents did in the preceding decades.[9] He will have to work more productively, probably for longer hours, and perhaps will have to rely on one or more off-farm incomes in the household. But if the farm enterprise can survive—a big "if" when world commodity prices are as low as they were in 1998—he will also produce greater wealth, as an individual and a household, than did his parents and grandparents. So the economic revolution goes, and so the Saskatchewan farm is caught up in the transition.

III

THESE IMPORTANT DECISIONS WERE not taken without consultation and debate. Saskatchewan, now as in the past, is a hotbed of political discussion. And it is a society undergoing rapid change, not just because of these developments in the farm economy but also because of the dramatic changes in the circumstances of Native Canadians.

The past three decades have seen intense debate in politics and sharp swings in party fortunes. The Blakeney New Democrats governed from 1971 to early 1982. They were soundly defeated by Grant Devine's Conservatives, whose two administrations lasted from 1982 to 1991. Roy Romanow's New Democratic Party government swept Devine from office in 1991 and obtained a renewed mandate in 1995. Thus, Saskatchewan has the unique distinction in North America of having been governed by social democrats for thirty-nine of the fifty-six years from 1944 to the end of the twentieth century.

Allan Blakeney led a government committed to greater local control over the economy. It relied on Crown-owned corporations on the grounds that they represented "a sure means of democratizing the economy"—that is, their direction was responsible to the people because it was accountable to the cabinet and the legislature, and because control over the corporations' decisions remained within the province. The alternative, Blakeney claimed, was control exercised elsewhere and, in all likelihood, on the basis of annual or even quarterly shareholder returns.[10] This defence of a "mixed economy," in which government, corporations and labour share in the planning of long-term industrial goals and economic transition, was typical of a man who believed strongly that the NDP's great strength was its commitment to "distributional justice . . . fair shares for all in a free society. We want a fairer tax system and we want to continue to offer a broad range of educational and health services."

This NDP administration lost power in 1981, a time of great economic uncertainty, when mortgage rates shot up to 23 percent

and the inflation rate was 12.5 percent. Blakeney said his government had lost touch with the unease among the middle classes in
the province and focused too single-mindedly on the conditions of
the less advantaged. The success of their government-owned
resource corporations, he told his biographer, led to "a perception
that our government was well off, but the people were not." The
Conservatives won 54 percent of the popular vote and fifty-six of
sixty-four seats in 1982, a landslide, and declared that Saskatchewan
was "open for business" just as Ross Thatcher had done when he
defeated the NDP in 1964."[11]

Grant Devine's government did spend more generously to aid
the middle classes, notably by ending the provincial tax on gasoline,
cutting personal income tax rates, putting a ceiling on mortgages
(the government would pay the difference between market rates
and a specified ceiling rate) and offering subsidized loans to young
farmers buying land. It also aided corporations by reducing the
royalties imposed on the oil, potash and uranium industries,
privatizing the highway-construction business (with a huge sell-off
of government-owned equipment), creating a subsidized share
purchase plan that encouraged local citizens to invest in local companies and offering a variety of subsidies for specific projects such
as a meat packing plant.

Devine's legislation illustrates the great gulf between the two
administrations. His Conservative government revised labour laws to
aid owners in their contests with workers, reduced spending on
women's programs, cut or abandoned affirmative action programs,
eliminated grants for certain international aid programs and lowered
welfare payments. Devine also "re-staffed" the civil service, a euphe-
mism employed in a book favourable to the government. Its authors,
Don Baron and Paul Jackson, claimed that Devine wished to "de-
politicize" the Crown corporations by replacing NDP nominees with
people from the private sector "who understood business and profit
and loss, and who were competent, sincere, and strong-willed."[12]

The Devine government tried to diversify the Saskatchewan
economy by encouraging the private sector. According to Baron and
Jackson, Devine "believed the people could invest more of their own
money to better advantage themselves, creating jobs and building
the province. He was determined to reduce taxes and let the people
keep more of their money." Far from gifts to corporations, Devine
offered "no grant, no subsidies. Just tax incentives." Outsiders might
have wondered about this unusual distinction. And Devine's

"biggest challenge," according to Baron and Jackson, "was the defeatism, the fear and the lack of confidence that reflects itself in the election of socialist governments."[13]

The Devine government ran large deficits. And it encountered tough economic times, partly due to its spending ways and partly due to the same decline in world commodity prices that had handicapped the Alberta government. Eventually it had to resort to drastic cuts in provincial expenditures. However, there was never a coherent system of public administration. Even Baron and Jackson concluded that Devine

> gave his cabinet ministers immense leeway in running their departments. No hands-on premier, Grant Devine.... Here were the seeds of trouble... [his] frenzy of activity left Devine little time to manage his own government. He sometimes failed to understand what his cabinet ministers were doing or trying to accomplish. Worse still, the staff he selected to manage his office and his government was often youthful and inexperienced when its greatest need was for maturity and judgment.[14]

In 1991 the Conservatives were unceremoniously removed from office in a sweep as profound as the one that had elected them ten years earlier. The Romanow NDP government then resumed the implementation of social democratic principles consistent with those of earlier New Democrat and Co-operative Commonwealth Federation (CCF) administrations. Though its tax increases and austerity measures were drastic, the New Democrats' financial restructuring turned around the deficit–debt spiral very quickly. The fate of the Saskatchewan Conservative party has not been pleasant to contemplate. Nine former MLAs have been convicted of fraud in an alleged scheme to circumvent legislative rules on the spending of communications allowances. The party has broken apart and some of its memebers have merged with former Liberals in a new Saskatchewan Party. The Devine government was unprepared for the discipline of power.[15]

The eternal battle between liberty and equality is obviously not over. For that is what is at stake in this cycle of party political fortunes. Those who praise the virtues of personal initiative and uncontrolled markets are today's advocates of a particular kind of liberty; those who emphasize state ownership in peripheral economies and greater redistribution of wealth stand for equality. These are matters of community priorities. The community, as a whole, must decide what it is prepared to accept and what it is willing to risk at any given moment in its history.

A crucial difference between the contemporary debate and that of earlier generations is the bitterness with which it is now conducted: the courtesy and goodwill towards opponents that was once so marked in political life (Tommy Douglas remarked on it in his last speech to the Saskatchewan legislature), has been replaced by howling and catcalling and abuse. Davey Steuart, a former Liberal leader, was shocked upon returning to the Saskatchewan assembly in the mid-1980s: "It was just unbelievable. . . . This hatred just built up. It's there."[16]

The stakes are no higher. The participants are not less intelligent. Rather, patience with disagreements over economic fundamentals and social priorities has disappeared. The bitterness is dangerous because it undermines the power of reasonable discussion in the wider society. Instead, it encourages extremism, the worst danger in parliamentary democracies. Thus, the vigour of Saskatchewan public debates, as in British Columbia, is both encouraging and worrying.

IV

First Nations issues press upon the provincial governments in western Canada, including the government of Saskatchewan, because conditions in many aboriginal communities are now intolerable. At a 1997 political convention in Saskatchewan, members of a Regina constituency introduced a resolution calling on the government to expand "co-op housing projects. . . . as a way to stabilize inner city neighbourhoods" in three of the province's largest cities. Premier Romanow's speech to that same party meeting described one of these districts, the West Flat in Prince Albert, as being "like too many of our inner city core areas: a place of little hope."[17]

It was near the West Flat that one of the most unpleasant incidents of racism in recent Prairie history occurred. On January 28, 1991, as dusk was giving way to darkness, Leo LaChance, a middle-aged Cree man from nearby Big River, dropped into a riverfront store west of the city's central business district, perhaps to sell some furs. The interior of this rickety building was piled high with small items for sale and a messy array of memorabilia, including Nazi

items. Its owner, a man said to be the Saskatchewan leader of the
Church of Jesus Christ Christian Aryan Nations, raised a semiauto-
matic rifle and fired several shots at him. Leo LaChance stumbled
out of the store onto River Street, lay in the snow until passersby
discovered him, and died several hours later in hospital.[18]

The case will never be understood completely. Prince Albert
citizens condemned the murderer and the wanton recklessness of his
act. However, the tensions unleashed by the LaChance murder
fuelled an atmosphere of crisis in the community. Such an atmosphere pervades Native Canadian relations with the larger society in
many parts of western Canada today.

Suspicion is rife. When one noted Saskatchewan artist, Edward
Poitras, who is Native Canadian, criticized another artist, Joe Fafard,
who is not, over the latter's public sculpture of a buffalo destined for
a prominent location in downtown Regina, Poitras explained the
issue as a struggle over non-aboriginal appropriation of the aboriginal past. Poitras especially denounced Fafard's wish to title the sculpture in Cree.[19]

Similarly, when a poll commissioned by the Federation of
Saskatchewan Indian Nations (FSIN) reached the Saskatoon and
Regina newspapers, the journalists assigned to the story took the
angle that an "overwhelming" proportion of Saskatchewan citizens
viewed aboriginal people in a negative light. Their stories cited epi-
thets such as greedy, dirty, crybabies, drunks and freeloaders to represent the purported views of Saskatchewan people and noted the
FSIN concern about the results. Yet the poll itself, it later transpired,
had discovered that only "a very small portion" of the citizenry
expressed negative views about aboriginal people. The furore, and
the confusion, illustrated the ambiguity in western race relations.[20]

Given the racial tensions, it is noteworthy that a Saskatchewan
court was the first in Canada to take advantage of a 1998 Supreme
Court ruling on racial bias in potential jurors. In their decision,
Canada's justices decided that jurors being empanelled could be
questioned about their racial views to, as a newspaper report put
it, "root out those whose prejudices could destroy the fairness
of a criminal trial." In the first application of this principle, a
Saskatchewan judge ruled that potential jurors in a murder case
would be subject to this kind of scrutiny. As he said, "Widespread
anti-aboriginal racism is a grim reality in Canada and in Saskatchewan. It exists openly and blatantly in attitudes and actions of
individuals. It exists privately in the fears, in the prejudices and

stereotypes held by many people and it exists in our institutions."
The Crown prosecutor in this trial approved of the judge's ruling:
"I think it will, if nothing else, give the accused person a sense that
if they belong to a visibly identifiable group they may get a fairer
trial. We are kind of leading the pack here—it's the first of its kind
in Saskatchewan and I'm sure other jurisdictions will follow
suit."[21]

Issues of aboriginal economic self-sufficiency preoccupy the citizens of Saskatchewan, as they do citizens in the other western
provinces. However, successive Saskatchewan governments have been
slow to address the completion of land allocations that had been
promised by Ottawa under the treaties signed in the late nineteenth
century. Some of the claims were nearly settled in 1980–81, but the
process was delayed when a few members of the NDP cabinet recognized that the expenditure would run into public opposition. The
Romanow government again raised the issue in the 1990s and soon
established standards for "treaty land entitlement" based upon current
population numbers. By early 1996 all twenty-eight bands that were
owed land under outstanding treaty promises had signed agreements
to purchase nearly two million acres (1.5 percent of the province),
with joint federal-provincial financing of over $500 million.[22]
The grants of land will be a century overdue when they are finally
completed.

Aboriginal issues are difficult in the present and they are only
going to become more so in the future. The Saskatchewan population is aging, but the aboriginal element within the total, now about
one in eight—is increasing rapidly. Its youthfulness and its high
birth rate have led to predictions that aboriginal people will soon be
challenging the century-long European dominance within the
province.[23] The danger, of course, is racial conflict.

Saskatchewan is the most open and consultative of the four
western provinces in the tenor of its public debates. Not that it is
alone in holding elections and debating public issues, but that its
decisions are most obviously reached *after* thorough public debate.
Discussion occurs not just in the legislature and the press but in conversations and in community institutions. One sees the difference in
the government's publications, which set out careful descriptions of
the circumstance—whether in hospital services or highway construction—and then offer costs and alternatives. The government
will choose, of course, but it will have ensured that the issue is
discussed thoroughly before it commits itself. The contrast with

Alberta, for example, where decisions come more quickly, and the government's publications explain what was done and why, rather than what might be done, illustrate what I mean by the vitality of Saskatchewan democracy. The province will need all of this openness, as well as wisdom and patience, as it addresses the social and economic issues of the next generation. Because the choices are so few, government is never easy in a small, peripheral community.

REFERENCES

1. Urban sixty-four percent, rural thirty-seven percent.

2. Saskatchewan Agriculture and Food, *Saskatchewan Agriculture: An International Field of Opportunity* (ca 1994); also *Saskatchewan: The Centre for Pork Opportunity* (ca 1996).

3. Barry Wilson, "Tallying the cost of the Crow's demise" and "World trade rules clip Crow's wings" *Western Producer* 9 April 1998, pp. 46, 47.

4. "Research and development: foundation for the future" *Western Grocer Magazine*, special supplement, Saskatchewan Food Report 1995, pp. 8–9.

5. Saskatchewan Agriculture and Food, *Agriculture Biotechnology Report* (ca 1996) pp. 6–10.

6. Saskatchewan Agriculture and Food *Saskatchewan: The Centre for Pork Opportunity* (ca 1996).

7. Ed White, "Hog agency begins life as private company" *Western Producer* 9 April 1998, p. 1.

8. Saskatchewan Highways and Transportation, *Investing in Transportation: A Transportation Strategy for Saskatchewan People* (1997).

9. Wilson, "Tallying the cost of the Crow's demise."

10. Dennis Gruending, *Promises to Keep: A Political Biography of Allan Blakeney* (Saskatoon: Western Producer Prairie Books 1990) p. 235.

11. Gruending, *Promises to Keep* pp. 220–25.

12. Don Baron and Paul Jackson, *Battleground: The Socialist Assault on Grant Devine's Canadian Dream* (Toronto: Bedford House Publishing 1991) p. 70.

13. Baron and Jackson, *Battleground* pp. 23, 43, 47. They write: "The Tories were people who bridled at the seemingly endless interference of government bureaucrats in their lives. They were people who were striving to create wealth and jobs and to build the province, and who wanted a social safety net that served

those in need without dulling initiative and creating costly bureaucracies." p. xv.

14. Baron and Jackson, *Battleground* p. 315.

15. "Tories decimated by fraud scandal: Four members of the caucus joined with four renegade Liberals to form new Saskatchewan party" *Calgary Herald* 24 August 1997, A6, 7.

16. L. D. Lovick, ed., *Tommy Douglas Speaks* (Vancouver: Douglas and McIntyre 1979) p. 145; Gruending, *Promises to Keep* p. 226: Steuart reported: "Blakeney got up to speak and it was just unbelievable. They wouldn't even let the guy get a word in edgewise. They were shouting at him from every side." This attitude was reflected on the other side of the House, too.

17. Resolution from Regina Elphinstone NDP constituency association to provincial convention, in *The Commonwealth* 57, 8 (November 1997) 38; Roy Romanow, "Convention 1997 Speech" *The Commonwealth* 58,1 (January 1998) 7.

18. Connie Sampson, *Buried in the Silence* (Edmonton: Newest Press 1995).

19. Greg Beatty, "The skeletons in Regina's cultural closet" *Globe and Mail* 16 May 1998, E4.

20. The *Regina Leader-Post* and *Saskatoon StarPhoenix* reports appeared on 26 February 1998. The issue was discussed in Maggie Siggins, "Mind how you read that survey" *Globe and Mail* 12 March 1998, A19.

21. David Roberts, "Racial-bias quiz a first for jurors at Saskatchewan trial: Process designed to weed out obvious bigots backed by Supreme Court ruling last month" *Globe and Mail* 18 July 1998, A3.

22. Gruending, *Promises to Keep* pp. 218–9; NDP polls reported that the people believed aboriginal bands were receiving too much from the government. Roy Romanow, then the attorney general, is said to have stalled the 1980–81 process. The process received a high priority under Romanow's new administration in the 1990s; Saskatchewan Indian and Métis Affairs Secretariat *Annual Report 1995–1996*.

23. One article predicted that Saskatchewan could be one-third aboriginal in less than fifty years; David Margoshes, "Saskatchewan faces change as aboriginal population booms" *Vancouver Sun* 18 July 1998, B1.

CHAPTER TEN

Manitoba

MANITOBA WAS KNOWN AS the "first new province of the Dominion" when it entered Confederation in 1870. Later, it was called the keystone province, both because of its shape after the 1912 boundary extension (an annexation of northern lands also granted Quebec and Ontario) and its location as the central locking stone in the arch of the nation. In the 1970s and 1980s it was "friendly Manitoba," its lively arts and music scene complemented by ethnic cuisine, folk festivals and a multicultural population. Since then, its capital city, Winnipeg, has tried two new slogans: "Gateway to the New West," in which it basks in the reflection of the Alberta and British Columbia booms; and "Terminus of the mid-continent trade corridor," a transportation-based concept of the NAFTA era that projects a trade route from Guadalajara, Mexico, through the American Midwest to Manitoba.[1] Neither of the recent Winnipeg slogans speak directly to the nature of Manitoba itself. Rather, they address the province as a threshold, a place to step over en route to somewhere else.

I

MANITOBA IS A MORE urban version of Saskatchewan. Its population is just a little larger than that of its Prairie neighbour (in 1997 1.15 million compared to Saskatchewan's 1.02 million) and it, too, accounts for about ten percent of the western population. Its capital city cannot compete with Vancouver, nor is it now in the same league as Calgary. Winnipeg was Canada's third-largest metropolis in the early years of the twentieth century, but has steadily lost areas of hinterland in the intervening years and is now Canada's eighth-largest.

Manitoba does have many strengths. Its economy is the most diverse of all the western provincial economies, its unemployment rate is usually lower than the national average (as in Saskatchewan, unemployed residents move to likelier job sites), and its relatively large urban centre sustains communications industries and cultural activities that are not as easily supported in the more dispersed communities of Saskatchewan or the Atlantic provinces.

Manitoba Exports by Selected Commodity Groups, 1995

Millions of Dollars

Agricultural Commodities	1465.2
Motor Vehicles	940.4
Mineral Products	736
Base Metals	477.7
Wood / Pulp & Paper	447.4
Machinery / Equipment	431.1
Processed Foods	388.6
Other	569.6

From *Final Task Force Report* (Manitoba Working for Value Task Force, 1997) p.15.

Two-thirds of Manitoba, above a southeast to northwest diagonal, is pre-Cambrian shield, the rock-and-lake country once scoured by retreating glaciers and now a home for mining prospectors, hydro engineers and some fishing and forestry activities, as well as for aboriginal households whose families have occupied the land for several thousand years. Along its northeast margin, the Hudson Bay lowland is extremely cold in winter and is best known for its natural features, including the flowers, birds, northern lights and polar bears that attract visitors from less-favoured climes. The population of this zone is less than ten percent of the provincial total.

One-sixth of the province's area, chiefly in the north, is covered by water. Thus, one can argue that Manitoba's chief resource in the longer term may be fresh water. At the moment, its rivers drive a number of hydroelectric turbines and its hydro potential accounts for seventy percent of the Prairie region's potential hydro capacity.

Manitoba's agricultural zone is much smaller than that of Saskatchewan. Its nineteen million acres of farmland, fourteen percent of the province's area, contrast with Saskatchewan's sixty-six million acres or forty-one percent of the area. Along the diagonal axis of the shield sit four giant lakes, Winnipeg, Manitoba, Winnipegosis and Cedar, reminders of the glacial sea, Lake Agassiz, that once covered the southern half of the province. Its lake-bed origin accounts for the remarkable flatness of much of this terrain. The Red River flood of 1997, the seventh such crisis in the past two centuries, illustrated the characteristics of this "flood-plain."

Manitoba has only a few smaller urban centres. Two mining towns, Thompson and Flin Flon, are located in the north, and two other mid-north service centres, The Pas and Swan River, supply lumber and farm operations in their districts. In the south, four centres of population ring the capital—Selkirk, Portage la Prairie, Steinbach and the region that embraces the towns of Morden, Winkler and Altona—and all have some industries and serve as extensions of the capital's economy and society.

In the agricultural southwest lies Manitoba's second city, Brandon, once a quiet university town and service centre but now booming towards a population of fifty thousand on the strength of a large pork-packing plant and associated economic growth.

Settlement in Winnipeg can trace its origins to a Scottish colonizing experiment at Red River undertaken by Lord Selkirk in 1811–12 and to the largely-Métis households, divided into Catholic and Protestant, French and English-speaking parishes, that cultivated parts of Selkirk's tract over the next fifty years. The city dominated Prairie trade and communications in the half-century after Confederation. It became a centre for the grain industry, a focus for finance and consumer goods, as well as education and publishing services, but its boom-time was brief. The subsequent seventy years of stability have left marks both positive and negative on this city of nearly 700,000.

The city is best known for its cultural activities, ranging from music and dance to film and literature, and for its historic ethnic diversity. Though the annual total of new immigrants pales in comparison to the recent rapid changes in Toronto and Vancouver, Winnipeg's ethnic variety stands out among Prairie cities. The emergence of large Filipino, Mennonite, and aboriginal communities in recent decades prompts thoughts of the historic challenges to British dominance of the province posed by Jewish, French, German, Icelandic, Ukrainian and Polish fractions around the turn of the twentieth century. Winnipeg is now, as it has been from its foundation, a city of ferment and conflict as well as conservatism.

II

RURAL MANITOBA, LIKE THE rest of the rural West, is undergoing rapid change and dislocation. Imagine that you have been working comfortably in the same occupation for years—the same trade or profession or craft—and that your family has specialized in this role for generations. Imagine further that members of your family have carried out these tasks in this very workplace and community for almost a century. Then, within the space of your adult life, arguments erupt about the structure of the entire industry, half your workmates depart in a downsizing, and you, one of those staying on, have to study a vast range of new specialized data and acquire a demanding new set of skills, and even then you are not certain from one day and season to the next whether you will be able to make a go of this vastly changed enterprise on which your household now depends.

This is the case on the Prairie farm. The challenge is most acute in Manitoba, where transportation costs have leaped higher than in the other provinces. Thus, the pressure to "go niche"—that is, to adopt narrower specialties and a wider range of income-producing options—has been most intense. Rural Manitobans have been living through a revolution of their own during this generation. Farm production accounted for about one-twentieth of the provincial economy in the early 1990s, half the proportion of the 1970s. However, the extraordinary transition in the rural economy of recent years is expanding the relevance of agriculture once again.

The processed and semiprocessed food products of the increasingly specialized farms are finding new markets outside the province and the country. The value of these "agrifood" exports has nearly doubled between 1988 and 1997. Shipments of canola and canola products now approach the value of wheat shipments. The new bywords are frozen potatoes (french fries), pork, dry peas, flaxseed and poultry. Barley exports have plummeted as the province itself requires more feed grain, and sugar beets have disappeared, probably forever. Thus, the surviving farm households are acquiring new skills and products.

The Manitoba farm exports described as "unprocessed," such as wheat, account for half the total. Those labelled "semi-processed," including canola and canola cake, cattle and hogs, peas and milled oats, represent one-third. The "processed" agrifood exports, including pork, beef, frozen potatoes, honey, dried egg yolks and skim milk powder, represent one-sixth.[2]

What is life like on the modern farm? During the year 1995–96, David Roberts wrote a weekly column for the *Globe and Mail* on the activities of one Manitoba farm family. Roberts described "the sense of wonder, peace and solitude that comes with each vibrantly changing season on the land." He also illustrated the adaptations of the modern rural household. He watched the raising of a thousand hogs and 35,000 chickens, the seeding of field crops and the use of herbicides and fertilizers, the excitement of the harvest weeks, the isolation imposed by a winter storm. And how did his hosts, the Brandt family, and their neighbours adapt to their new circumstances? At one point in the year, their

> good fortune with pigs seemed to be in jeopardy. The Manitoba government had announced an end to the "single-desk" system by which all hogs are sold through a marketing board. This subject was well examined by farming friends who gathered at a restaurant in Steinbach to solve the world's problems. They came from neighbouring towns and villages such as Blumenort, New Bothwell and Kleefeld. And the talk among these young farmers, men who are as comfortable in front of a computer as they are inside a hog barn, was loose, polite, and generally filled with optimism.[3]

The pressure to change originates not just in abstract theory or daily economics, but in lectures delivered by government representatives. A Manitoba government committee of 1997 entitled, significantly, the "Working for Value Task Force," aimed to encourage value-added processing and a diversified range of exports. Such goals could be achieved, committee members concluded, only if an "entrepreneurial spirit and attitude" was cultivated in the educational system and in all adult training:

> A change in attitude is needed in many areas so that rural residents can assume a greater role in determining their economic future. In short, rural Manitobans must take a stronger leadership role in diversifying their economy and adding value to the things they produce. Trying to foster a major shift in thinking—whether in an individual or in a community—can be difficult. Yet without a profound change in attitude, the long-term competitiveness and viability of our province's economy will be threatened.

The committee report addressed rural young people directly: they "must understand that they cannot wait for others to create jobs and wealth in their communities; they must instead be prepared to create their own opportunities." The committee stressed the market for farm tourism, the need for local equity capital pools and the need for research-and-development projects that were "more market driven." Of course, it also repeated time-honoured injunctions about the need for better roads.[4] Meanwhile, young Manitobans left for greener pastures in "the city" (Brandon or Winnipeg), or in the other big cities of the West.

The exodus continues because, even after adapting successfully, and occupying the new niche markets, not all the potential farmers can make a living on the modern farm. Even the criteria for the Outstanding Young Farmer Program include a clause that nominees "must earn only two-thirds of their income from their farming operation to qualify." In short, rural households require off-farm income if they are to thrive. The 1998 winners, Tom and Cindy Kieper, raise purebred cattle, forage and field crops on a fifth-generation farm near Russell, Manitoba, but they also rely on off-farm income.[5]

The pivotal Manitoba institution in the traditional grain economy has been Manitoba Pool Elevators, the province's largest co-operative. It has 16,000 members and controls just over half the elevator-storage capacity and grain-handling activity in the province. It also owns a chain of seventy-three sales outlets for fertilizers and herbicides, much of which it produces in subsidiaries. Formed in 1925 as a farmer-owned elevator system, the pool has expanded in recent years into oilseed crushing, the milling of oats, the manufacturing of frozen foods, and the marketing of livestock. It also owns part of a private firm that exports grain, oilseeds and specialty crops.[6]

Yet even an enterprise with seven hundred employees and gross revenues of $1.4 billion was not sufficiently large to maintain a secure foothold in the rapidly changing farm economy. In July 1998 Manitoba Pool and the slightly larger Alberta Pool agreed to merge. Facing giant competitors in every sphere of their activities, the farmer delegates who governed the two co-operatives revised the exclusive provincial mandates that had ruled their operations. Said a delegate from Birtle, Manitoba: "If we have to play ball against these major-league hitters coming in, in order to compete we have to get bigger."[7] Agricore, the merged Manitoba–Alberta Pool co-operative, will remain exclusively farmer-owned. It is the last grain-handling co-op to hold this status.

Two other strategies have been employed by other Canadian grain companies. United Grain Growers, at one time a farmer-owned company, rejected a merger with the pools and, instead, sold forty-two percent of its stock to the American conglomerate, Archer-Daniels-Midland. Saskatchewan Wheat Pool, the largest Prairie grain-handling firm, after a searching debate among its members, undertook a historic shift in policy by selling shares on the Toronto Stock Exchange in an initial public offering of $153 million. Interestingly, new Saskpool investors could buy only non-voting shares. Active farmer members alone could hold voting shares. This is yet another route from the old co-operative to the new agrarian capitalism.

The reasons for the changes include the invasion of large international firms such as ConAgra, Dreyfus and Cargill, and the marketing efficiencies associated with larger corporations. The old grain companies needed large pools of capital to undertake expensive restructuring. If they did not reorganize quickly, they would be left behind by the rapid developments in the grain-handling and farm-service system.[8]

Again, one meets the pressure for change in rural Manitoba. It affects most institutions and individuals.

III

Northern Manitoba might seem relatively insulated from the pressures in the south. The mines and forests and hydro sites continue according to processes and rules that have been in place for more than a generation. But there, too, the new ways have assaulted the old. First Nations people have felt the pressures of the outside world most keenly.

Of the one hundred thousand people in the North, half are aboriginal and half are not. The latter, mainly resident in industrial communities, have road access to the south. Thirty-five aboriginal communities, however, rely on airplanes and often inadequate landing strips for regular connections to the rest of the world. Their freight has to await the "winter roads," the remarkable ice technology that has evolved in the past two generations, for the shipment of goods in truckload quantities. In the mid-1980s, according to a Manitoba study, aboriginal household incomes in the North were about sixty percent of the provincial average. Income from employment alone, excluding transfer payments and locally harvested food, clothing and shelter materials, was less than forty percent of the average income levels in the North.[9]

A Manitoba government commission concluded in 1993, as had Saskatchewan and Alberta planners, that aboriginal bands were still owed land grants from treaties that had been signed eighty to a hundred years earlier. Not surprisingly, the commissioners suggested that the process be expedited. This unfinished business had been taken up in the 1970s, and a tentative agreement on how to proceed was signed by government and First Nations representatives in 1983. About one million acres will be transferred to aboriginal control, supported by a federal government grant of $76 million. The first two land-entitlement packages were finally approved by band votes in 1998.[10]

The 1993 government commission encouraged expansion of appropriate "resource development activities" in the North. These included fishing, trapping and ecotourism. It also recommended improved educational opportunities. However, as a member of the Opasquia Cree Nation told the commissioners, the obstacles to development were numerous: "While the North may be perceived as a pristine tourist paradise, full of uncharted wilderness, there are real problems. We have unemployment rates approaching ninety percent on many reserves and communities, and the problems bred by unemployment, such as alcoholism, family violence, high suicide rates and lower life expectancies, are very real and visible in the North."[11]

In the past two decades, large numbers of northern First Nation and Métis people have left their homes for Winnipeg. The number of aboriginal people in Manitoba's capital is much debated, but in 1998 it certainly was in the range of fifty to sixty thousand. These citizens are represented by city councillors and members of the provincial legislature in the conventional manner. However, their own organizations, the Assembly of Manitoba Chiefs and the Manitoba Métis Federation, find it difficult to represent their interests consistently because both are also responsible for rural and northern aboriginal communities. An Aboriginal Council of Winnipeg grew up in the 1990s in an attempt to fill the gap. The political problems it faces—within aboriginal circles, as well as in the wider community—are far from being resolved.[12]

The range of aboriginal social issues is difficult to grapple with. Where should policy planners begin? One major Manitoba initiative was the Aboriginal Justice Inquiry (AJI) of 1988–91. Conducted by Associate Chief Justice A.C. Hamilton, a non-aboriginal, and Associate Chief Judge C.M. Sinclair, an aboriginal of Anishnabe heritage, this commission was launched as a result of two incidents related to law enforcement. First, a trial in The Pas, sixteen years after the murder of Helen Betty Osborne, an aboriginal schoolgirl, resulted in the conviction of only one of four defendants, though all four were said to be present when she was killed and though there allegedly had been widespread local gossip about the details of her death shortly after it occurred. Second, a Winnipeg police officer shot an aboriginal leader during a late-night encounter on a city street and was quickly exonerated by an internal police department review.

The AJI, appointed by Howard Pawley's New Democrat government, was asked to re-examine both incidents. It was also invited to go far beyond them and to consider all the Manitoba legal processes, from policing to courts, jails and welfare support, in relation to aboriginal people.

The judges' long and ambitious analysis tackled aboriginal circumstances in Manitoba as an issue of government and law. It argued that aboriginal self-government should be officially recognized, that is, the report urged the federal and provincial governments to acknowledge "the right of Aboriginal communities to run their own affairs within their own territory." The judges proposed the establishment of aboriginal courts and justice systems in aboriginal communities on an incremental basis, commencing with summary-conviction criminal cases and child-welfare issues. They also urged the completion of treaty land entitlement deals and called for an Aboriginal Claims Tribunal to hear other sorts of claims against the government.

The report was unusually sweeping. The judges advocated the foundation of aboriginal-controlled police forces for the reserves. They opposed incarceration except as a penalty of last resort and expressed a preference for local aboriginal sentencing panels and innovative sentences. They called for swift action on family violence and abuse, expansion of aboriginal child-welfare agencies, new approaches to aboriginal young offenders, inclusion of aboriginal people on Manitoba juries, improved cross-cultural educational programs and a strong affirmative action program to place aboriginal people in positions of responsibility throughout the justice system.[13]

The report constituted one positive and carefully considered approach to the dilemma of rapid cultural and economic change being experienced by First Nations people. It put law and government at the forefront of the adaptation process and placed great responsibility on a small group of aboriginal political leaders. It was a bold and, in the Canadian context, innovative proposal. But it was not, in the end, given a chance to work.

The AJI report was received by the Conservative administration that had come to power in the interim. Premier Gary Filmon wanted to reduce the role of government in public affairs. He sought to liberate private enterprise. He thought in terms of economic problems, not legal or parliamentary institutions. He and his cabinet conceived of export growth as the solution to Manitoba's concerns. The AJI report and its proposed means of tackling aboriginal issues was shelved, just as many aboriginal witnesses had prophesied.[14] A decade later, all the issues discussed by the AJI commissioners remain.

A national crime report based on 1997 records placed Manitoba at the top of the tables, as measured by the numbers of violent crimes per one hundred thousand people. Manitoba led all the provinces in weapons offences, motor vehicle thefts, robberies, assault (non-sexual) and mischief. Of the nine largest cities, only Vancouver had a higher crime rate than Winnipeg, and the Manitoba capital led all cities in each of the above five categories. As in the studies conducted by the AJI a decade earlier, Manitoba's aboriginal people figured disproportionately in these offences. Did government policy choices contribute to this social disintegration?

IV

MANITOBA'S CAPITAL REGION, THE province's great strength—with agriculture—in the twentieth century, has not provided the economic and cultural leadership in recent years that it once did. Winnipeg's most publicized disappointment was the loss of a National Hockey League team, the Winnipeg Jets, but the city's economy, planning and rates of violent crime and urban poverty are probably of greater long-term significance. This is a city in search of a role. It badly requires policy innovation. It has found neither in the 1990s.

The departure of a sports franchise, even a franchise in one of the continent's major sports leagues, is not the end of civilized society. But the loss of the Jets in 1996 did hit the city hard. It confirmed a thought that had been slowly crystallizing in the preceding years: the community is relatively less prominent, less prosperous and less attractive to outsiders than its leading western competitors. As an editorial in the *Free Press* said, "The city suffers from a reputation, unfair as it may be, that it is a boring place to live, even among its own citizens."[15]

A regular columnist on spiritual affairs, Karen Toole-Mitchell, reported on a series of calls to a radio show expressing the view that the city was "sad." She wrote that the city was, indeed,

> suffering from a deep spiritual sadness. What I am writing about is our concern and connections as a community. What I am writing about is our daily communion of compassion, equality and justice with each other. Some of us may well be very happy and content, but is it not at the expense of those who are not?

She then discussed poverty in the city and likened it to conditions in 1911 when J.S. Woodsworth, famous social reformer and founder of a social democratic political party, wrote a tract, *My Neighbour*, on these very issues.[16]

A report about Winnipeg by Gerald Flood that appeared in the *Vancouver Sun* struck the same theme but with different evidence. Manitoba has consistently lost population, especially young people, to other provinces. According to a Statistics Canada report, the numbers of those departing surpassed new arrivals by 55,000 in the decade 1987–97. Manitoba gained in total population only because the aboriginal birthrate was high and because of international immigration. People continue to leave, according to Flood, for the simple reason that the city seems dull. A video producer who returned to his hometown, Winnipeg, was a rarity. Why did he do so? In Winnipeg, he said, he and his young family were able to enjoy a far more attractive life than was possible in Vancouver. He saw the lower house prices, the length of the drive to work, the cottage in lake country and the cultural institutions of the city as great advantages. Yet, despite this positive testimony, Flood's report returned to the city's "dull image":

> Exactly why people are staying away in droves is unclear. Part of the answer is that provincial economies across Canada, especially the three Prairie provinces, are doing well, so there's little incentive to move from one to another. But many fear part of the reason is a national perception that "Winterpeg" is in decline, that for too long it lived by its reputation as a cultured city with a thriving arts community and failed to notice that no one much cared.[17]

What went wrong? Part of the story was that city and province, as we have seen, experienced a transition that was inevitable for a peripheral region in a restructuring North American and international economy. In this restructuring, some industries were lost (meatpacking left Winnipeg, for example), and others, like farming, underwent dramatic change. In such periods, communities always hope that they will emerge in more or less the same relative position that they enjoyed previously—the same access to opportunity, the same economic standing and property values, the same amenities. Even if destined not to grow rich on an urban real estate bubble, they still hope they don't grow poorer.

Winnipeg did grow poorer, however, relative to the rest of the country and the continent. But this process had been going on for seventy years. Why should it suddenly seem more poignant? Both the provincial government, post–1988, and the Winnipeg government, post–1992, were budget-cutting, anti-public sector administrations. Hands-off, laissez-faire governments refuse to tackle social problems because they believe in the virtues of markets, the role of families as social welfare providers and the discipline of work—not the power of public institutions—as the means of shaping a community. If you want a vibrant community, these political leaders say, do it on your own. Rely on the private sector to deliver wise economic choices.

Some issues, however, governments alone can address. One, as I have noted, is the matter of an aboriginal cultural transition of enormous difficulty. In both Manitoba and Saskatchewan, this is a subject of pivotal importance because of the changing population balance. Manitoba, thus far, has ducked the challenge and, indeed, in reducing special postsecondary education programs for aboriginal people and the urban poor, has probably compounded its problems. This, I suspect, is one part of an answer to Mr. Flood.

A second answer arises from what a community does to establish and maintain a positive atmosphere during times of change. This is where the Jets come in. The battle to keep the hockey team was probably the single most watched issue of public policy in Winnipeg in the 1990s. Vast resources, measured by newspaper-column inches, the number of locally produced television news items, the time of business community volunteers and the emotional involvement of ordinary citizens went into the struggle. In one extraordinary week at the climax of the battle in May 1995, a public subscription raised $12 million; to put this into perspective, the United Way, which is organized as precisely and thoroughly as any military campaign, raises $9–10 million annually.

Why did the Save the Jets saga end in disaster? Surely part of the answer lies in the policies of the league. The National Hockey League had decided to enter the high-budget business culture of American professional sports. This transition, which occurred in the mid-1990s, just when Winnipeg's troubles came to a head, caused team budgets to skyrocket. The franchises had to rely increasingly on television revenues, which were obviously greater in larger markets. Moreover, in terms of privately held wealth, Winnipeg was closer to Quebec City, which also lost its hockey franchise, and to Saskatoon, which failed in a bid to buy a team, than to Ottawa or Vancouver, which managed to sustain franchises in the NHL. Winnipeg simply does not have as much money, whether in the pockets of ordinary ticket buyers or in corporate entertainment budgets, as Edmonton and Calgary.

It may seem that Winnipeg's only response is that of Saskatchewan poet Stephen Scriver:

so what it all comes down to
is that Yankee Board of Governors
don't know if their butts
is punched, bored, or shot out
by the Lone Ranger an none of em
better show their faces in Saskatchewan
or they'll have a half ton
ridin their tails all the way
from Moosomin to Maple Creek[18]

It's just a poem, of course. An expression of disappointment. The grapes were probably sour anyway. But menace and abuse are not normally viewed as responsible public debate. Is there no more constructive response to be made?

I believe there is a lesson to be learned from the Jets debacle. When communities make important decisions, frank public discussion is essential. Typically, when large public sums are involved, Her Majesty's government and Loyal Opposition are mobilized on either side of the question. Further, an independent media—the fourth estate, which so trumpets its social responsibility ethos—is also mobilized. Advocates of various public priorities present their arguments, the public acts as audience and critic, and the debate itself enables the participants to accept the eventual decision.

What nonsense. How naïve can one be? An election was in the offing in the spring of 1995. No government policy was ever announced. The provincial government won a renewed mandate on the shrewd, if ambiguous, claim that it would both limit public expenditure and save the Jets. Privately—outside the public forum—it whispered, exclusively in the ears of those eager to hear the message, that the needs of the Jets would be met and the team would stay in town.[19]

One can find reason to congratulate the people of Winnipeg, both business leaders and ordinary citizens, for their willingness to follow the debate and to contribute to the team. But Jim Silver, who campaigned against the investment of public funds in arena and franchise, concluded that the debate had not been open and fair. In his summary of this extraordinary episode in city history, he made an important observation about Winnipeg's atmosphere of negativism:

[I]t is probable that those cities that give voice to a
wide variety of ideas about how to build communities battered by powerful economic forces will be

the most likely to give birth to the creative energy that will generate economic and social vitality. This story of the struggle over the Jets suggests that Winnipeg is *not* now an environment in which such creativity is encouraged.[20]

Perhaps this is the second response to Gerald Flood's perceptive observation that the city had an apparently thriving arts scene about which "no one much cared." If one's arts and cultural institutions —and, in this context, newspapers and television news programs and public debates are cultural institutions—do not express the clearest and deepest debates within a community, then that community is indeed in danger of losing its soul. Silver believed that his group's position, at least, had not been given a fair share of public attention.

The failure of political and cultural institutions in one moment of challenge need not mark the province forever. There is always another tomorrow and another debate.

The positive side of contemporary Manitoba is that jobs do exist. The unemployment rate has been relatively low compared to the national level for almost two decades. Important local corporations cry out for trained workers. It is said that the city lacks garment workers, aerospace workers, computer technologists, truck drivers, electricians and building-trades workers. Such bright spots as film and the medical sciences, manufacturing and printing, agrifood and transportation, suggest that the province and the capital city will find economic growth, if not the utopia of pre–1914 dreams, in the future.

The recent failure lies in the refusal of governments, metropolitan and provincial, to tackle the obvious problems that surround it. It also lies in the failure of its major cultural institutions, as well as of its leaders, to debate what the plans and goals should be. The capital region is crying out for a planning policy. The aboriginal population and the northern transition must be addressed directly. Rural Manitoba is growing and changing more quickly than most of the province's citizens realize. Manitoba could use a dose of political frankness.

REFERENCES

1. City of Winnipeg, "Winnipeg into the New Millennium" (1998).

2. *Agricultural exports from Manitoba,* 1997 (in millions of dollars). Unprocessed exports = 52%; semiprocessed = 36%; processed = 12%.

Grains	773M
Oilseeds	443M
Live animals	405M
O/seed product	220M
Veg/legumes	198M
Red meat	158M
Grain products	55M
Seeds (sowing)	36M
Animal feeds	28M
Flax	26M
Fruit/nut	17M
Poultry, eggs	12.6M
Honey	8.9M
Animal products	4M
Dairy products	3.5M
Total	2,382M

Manitoba Agriculture Economics Branch, *Manitoba Agri-Food Exports* 1991–1997 (1998); and *Manitoba Agricultural Statistics* 1997; Canada West Foundation, *Agri-Food West: Renewal of Food Processing in Western Canada* (1997); Patrick G. Enright and R. G. Ironside, *Agri-Processing Industries as a Vehicle for Rural Development: Two Alberta Case Studies* (Brandon University, Rural Development Institute 1998); Thomas J. McEwen and Richard C. Rounds, *Issues relating to value-added processing of agricultural products in Manitoba* (Brandon University, Rural Development Institute 1994).

3. David Roberts, "On the Farm: A land for four seasons" *Globe and Mail* 6 February 1996, A6.

4. Manitoba, *Final Task Force Report: Working for Value* (1997) pp. 24, 25–40.

5. Laura Rance, "If you're a young farmer, you're outstanding" *Winnipeg Free Press*, 6 June 1998, B12; Ken Bessant with Richard Rounds and Erasmus Monu, *Off-Farm Employment in Agro-Manitoba* (Brandon University, Rural Development Institute 1993).

6. Manitoba Pool, *A Profile of Manitoba Pool Elevators 1925–1996* (1996).

7. Tracy Tjaden, "Grain co-ops propose tying the knot" *Winnipeg Free Press* 16 July 1998, A1–2.

8. Oliver Bertin, "Merger of pools would form giant" and "Co-ops keep corporate philosophy alive" *Globe and Mail* 29 December 1988, B1; also Ed White, "Sask Pool to ring in New Year with share offering" *Western Producer* 31 August 1995; Laura Rance, "Turf war sees pools vying for position" *Winnipeg Free Press* 11 April 1998 B12; Mathew Ingram, "Upheaval in the grain market," "UGG wins battle but war goes on" and "Wheat pools look to the future" *Globe and Mail* 11 March, 20 March 1997 and 27 April 1998, B2; Bill Redekopp, "Threatened pools begin merger talks" *Winnipeg Free Press* 22 April 1998, B6; Canadian Press, "Manitoba, Alberta wheat pools to merge" *Vancouver Sun* 1 August 1998, H4.

9. Northern Manitoba Economic Development Commission, *Northern Manitoba Sustainable Economic Development: A Plan for Action* (Winnipeg 1993) pp. 34–5.

10. Bud Robertson, "Band accepts treaty package; plans major land purchase" *Winnipeg Free Press* 16 July 1998, A7; the two 1998 deals involved the Rolling River First Nation north of Brandon and the Brokenhead Ojibway Nation north of Winnipeg. The latter deal, which included $3.6 million in federal money, will purchase over 14,000 acres of land. This will double the size of the present reserve, which claims 1,200 members, half non-resident, and which was set up under Treaty #1 of 1871.

11. Northern Manitoba Economic Development Commission, *Public Consultation Process* (Winnipeg 1993) B-8. The commission's main recommendations, the creation of a Resource Industry Council and a Northern Sustainable Economic Development Board, have not been implemented.

12. Stevens Wild, "Native leaders at odds over $12M complex" *Winnipeg Free Press* 22 June 1998.

13. The AJI hearings process also enabled many aboriginal people in remote communities to come into contact with government processes. One result was greater aboriginal willingness to express publicly what they had experienced during the past century. The revelations about government and church-run residential schools in Manitoba commenced shortly after. The saddest community story to emerge, and it too was presented to the AJI commissioners, has been described in Ila Bussidor and Ustun Reinart, *Night Spirits: The Relocation of the Sayisi Dene* (Winnipeg: University of Manitoba Press 1997).

14. A.C. Hamilton and C.M. Sinclair, *The Justice System and Aboriginal People* volume 1, p. 641, and *The Deaths of Helen Betty Osborne and John Joseph Harper* volume 2 of the *Report of the Aboriginal Justice Inquiry of Manitoba* (Winnipeg: Queen's Printer 1991).

15. "Little Comfort" *Winnipeg Free Press*, 8 July 1998, A10.

16. Karen Toole-Mitchell, "Winnipeg is suffering a deep spiritual sadness" *Winnipeg Free Press* 26 April 1998.

17. Gerald Flood, "A need to provide sends family back to Winnipeg" *Vancouver Sun* 20 June 1998, B1–2. Flood notes that Saskatchewan lost 93,000 people between 1987 and 1997.

18. Stephen Scriver, "Nobody Cares Who's Got the Blues" in *100% Cracked Wheat*, ed., Robert Currie et al (Moose Jaw: Coteau Books 1983) pp. 54–55

19. Jim Silver's *Thin Ice: Money, Politics, and the demise of an NHL Franchise* (Halifax: Fernwood Publishing 1996) tells the story of the Jets' demise.

20. Silver, *Thin Ice* p. 177.

Part III

Two Political Paths

CHAPTER ELEVEN

Coming to Terms with Diversity

POLITICAL DECISIONS AND POLITICAL parties are too complex and too changeable to fit the neat patterns that any ordinary observer craves. We, the public, are so eager for improvement, or at least action, that we don't permit the main actors in our political dramas to sit still long enough for a proper generalization to form. Nevertheless, I believe there are tendencies—patterns of thought and behaviour—in any political system. After all, the options available to the participants in a debate are usually limited to a very few. In making choices, which is what we ask of our political leaders, the parties select from this handful of options. The party choices, when looked at across the entire range of policy areas, tend to crystallize into a point of view, even a philosophy. These schools of thought are the subject of the following chapters.

The country has changed radically in ethnic composition over the past twenty-five years. The five largest western Canadian cities, like Toronto and Montreal in eastern Canada, have borne most of this dramatic restructuring in ethnic composition. The consequence has been a West sharply divided on issues of immigration, race and aboriginal policy.

I

VANCOUVER AND TORONTO ARE in the vanguard of Canada's multiracial transition. In each city, about thirty percent of the inhabitants of the metropolitan region belong to visible minorities. And though the proportions are smaller in Calgary, Edmonton and Winnipeg, these three cities are sufficiently a part of this trend that their residents, too, have had to adjust to a new social reality in a very short time. One Toronto newspaper editorial declared: "The latest census figures confirm what you know just from looking around: Canada is embarked upon a bold experiment. In the space of a few years, we have become a multiracial society, especially in our major cities."[1]

In 1971 it was estimated that about three percent of Canadians were not European in origin and most of these were aboriginal. In the 1996 census 11.2 percent were counted as part of a visible minority, and this did not include the large aboriginal component of western Canadian society.

Of these three million Canadians, 26.9 percent were Chinese and 21 percent were from South Asia (mainly from India and Pakistan). In addition, 17.9 percent were Black, 7.7 percent were Arab, and a similar proportion, 7.3 percent, were Filipino; 5.4 percent were Southeast Asian (from Cambodia, Vietnam, Laos and Indonesia), and a similar proportion, 5.5 percent, were Latin American.

The ethnic mix is slightly different in each major city. Toronto has nearly equal proportions of Chinese, South Asian and Black. In contrast, about half of Vancouver's visible minorities are Chinese, more than a quarter-million Chinese in total (about fifteen percent of the 1.8 million residents in the census district), and it is home as well to over 100,000 South Asians. Thus, ninety percent of its visible minorities come from some part of Asia. Vancouver possesses a much smaller proportion, relative to Toronto or Montreal, of Black Canadians. Winnipeg has a large proportion of aboriginal people and Filipinos, Calgary of Chinese and South Asians, and both have Latin American communities.

What matters is that the western cities have had to adjust rapidly to urgent and expensive demands, especially in schools and social services, whereas residents in the rest of each province have experienced less contact with the newcomers. Such disparities in experience create social and political divides.

11

THE VANCOUVER AIRPORT ALWAYS appears green and the pools of water on the runway verge never seem to dry up. Winter bound citizens from the rest of Canada reach the exit on the arrivals level thinking gratefully of cedar forests and warm rains. On one recent occasion, I reached the traffic circle with such thoughts in mind, only to be overwhelmed by the honking of horns and a parade of cars, many of them covered with hand-lettered protest signs. The traffic jam lasted for several hours, delaying recent arrivals and forcing would-be travellers to walk considerable distances from the nearest accessible drop-off points.

What was going on? The tendency in the rapidly expanding pool of gossip at the arrivals concourse was to blame the most obvious culprit—a group of taxi drivers, their cars stalled, horns blaring, signs proclaiming "No more tax" and "Have taken English class." They were from the Asian subcontinent (eighty percent of all the drivers, I learned later) and they were alleged to speak very little English, to know little of the geography of the districts they served, to operate poorly maintained vehicles and to appear brusque in manner. All this could be picked up in the hour or two that a recent arrival had to wait for a ride to the city centre.

Such generalizations were probably the normal reaction of a North American airport crowd: blame the worker in an industrial conflict. But there was a tinge of race hostility, too: blame the immigrant, the newcomer from Asia. For the visitor to Vancouver, the next step—to say that this city had a race problem—might seem an easy one.

Television news coverage of the disruption reinforced this easy conclusion. The news clips tended to favour the Airport Authority simply because the film footage presented the obvious fact that the workers had initiated the inconvenience. The clip also permitted the airport representative to deliver a few words of calm reason.

Yet, when I turned to the newspapers for further evidence, I was struck by the sympathy and balance of the stories. The *Vancouver Sun's* main analysis concentrated on the gruelling workweek and minimal earnings of one driver and explained his view of the Airport Authority's attempt to impose new rules upon his workplace without negotiation: he would lose more than he could afford—$3,500 from an already strained family budget of $12,000–15,000 a year—to pay the airport to administer activities that already functioned, in his view, reasonably well.

The *Province* reported the views of the two sides in brief and left its main observation to an opinion piece by Peter Clough. The essence of Clough's piece was that cabbies would soon be more regulated than anyone "this side of dentistry" and that the detail in the new regulations, especially on the colour and style of shirts and

trousers, was absurd. "I mean, really. We need dress codes for cabbies? Would it be all that shocking for some jet-lagged visitor to step
into a Vancouver cab and find that the driver's wearing . . . a polo
neck?"[2]

This episode illustrates the cultural context of daily life. Listen
to a reasonably well-off crowd that travels by air and has been incon-
venienced, and you will hear some rude, anti-worker sentiments.
Watch the television news and you will actually see evidence that taxi
drivers of South Asian heritage are causing disruption and noise; you
will hear perhaps a hundred words or so from the reporter at the
scene. But the visuals are far more eloquent. In other words, television news and airport gossip will prompt an unthinking response
to any social conflict.

By contrast, read the comments of the print reporters, who did
a little research, had the relative leisure to explain the situation in
250 words (in each of the two *Province* stories) or even 500 words
(the *Sun*), and who have had some years of experience as journalists. You will reach a different conclusion not only about a labour-
management dispute in one workplace but also about race relations
in a society.

Western Canada is no more the home of systemic, widespread
racism than is Ontario, Quebec or any other Canadian community.
Nor is it a society accustomed only to expressions of sweetness and
light. But western Canadians have done a great deal in the past
twenty-five years to make relations among ethnic groups smoother.
The extensive efforts to cultivate intergroup harmony in public education have undoubtedly borne fruit. Multicultural festivals such as
Winnipeg's Folklorama play a huge role in explaining each group to
the others. In the end, however, jobs, labour laws, careful reporting
in the media and frank political debate are a crucial part of the race
relations equation. In adjudicating these discussions and monitoring
popular opinion, the political parties have offered several options to
western Canadians.

III

JOBS FOR THESE NEWCOMERS (and their children, for one in three of
the visible minority Canadians was born in Canada) and discrimination in employment have become political issues. So has the entire
principle known as affirmative action. The Liberals and New
Democrats, both of whom have supported affirmative action, and

the Conservative and Reform parties, both opponents, represent the alternative views.

Deepak Obhrai, who is of South Asian heritage and grew up in Tanzania, moved to Canada twenty years ago and is now the multi-culturalism critic for the Reform Party in the House of Commons. He joins his party in opposing government-sponsored employment equity programs that seek to ensure equal access to jobs for members of visible minority groups. The Reform policy also opposes government aid for activities that preserve ethnic cultures. Preston Manning, leader of the Reform Party, personally inserted this paragraph into a party statement:

> If Canadians wish to preserve and develop a Canadian mosaic, Reformers advocate a new division of responsibility for doing so. It should be the responsibility of individuals, private organizations, and if necessary, local levels of government to provide and polish the pieces of the mosaic. The federal government should be responsible for providing the common background and glue which keeps the mosaic together by upholding personal freedoms and enforcing common values.[3]

The federal Liberal government, which permitted the introduction of a question on visible minority group membership in the 1996 census, has supported a wide variety of multicultural programs. This began with the announcement of a national multicultural policy in 1971 and was extended by former prime minister Trudeau's decision to include clauses in the 1982 Charter of Rights and Freedoms calling for the charter to be interpreted in a way that "preserves and enhances the multicultural heritage of Canada."

The charter guarantees equal protection and equal benefit of the law to all Canadians. Every citizen is supposed to be able to live free from discrimination on the basis of race, national or ethnic origin, colour or religion. The charter also permits positive measures to ameliorate disadvantages experienced by individuals or groups.

This "affirmative action" clause has been the subject of debate. Members of some right-wing political movements have argued that its ostensible goal of equality of opportunity has become, instead, equality of outcome. This defeats the valuable role of competition and market forces, they claim, and introduces unfairness and inefficiency into public choices.

Patrick Basham, one of the opponents of "reverse discrimination" (note this shift in terminology from "affirmative action") writes that: "race should not determine who gets into a school or who gets a job. . . . race should play *no* role in the way government recruits, employs or delivers services." Rather, he suggests, minorities require simply greater access to investment capital, more competition in the education system, fewer welfare payments and privatized public housing:

> The irony is that, under state-mandated preferences, one's biology and skin colour determine one's destiny. But why base someone's credentials upon his or her immutable physical characteristics? Above all, public policy in matters of race should be guided by the principle of nondiscrimination. The state cannot show a preference for one skin colour without discriminating against another.[4]

Both sides in this discussion profess to be motivated by a concern for fairness: those who favour affirmative action see entrenched discrimination that only quotas and targets will help to redress, whereas those who prefer market principles argue that free and open competition alone will treat everyone equally.

An illustration of these differences in everyday politics can be drawn from the Manitoba debate over what are known as "access" programs. The educational policy of the New Democratic Party governments included special provisions for aboriginal people, immigrants, northerners and single women who might benefit from further education but had been unable to enroll because of their *social* circumstances. The experiment included sustained counselling and support services, special funding and extended interviews with applicants to ensure careful selection. The program was a remarkable success and produced many hundreds of committed graduates. The dropout rate was, not surprisingly, low.

When a Conservative administration replaced the New Democrats in 1988, and the federal Conservative government cut back on its budget commitments, the program was sharply reduced. Now First Nations students who can bring their own band funding to the educational institution are the main recipients of the few remaining access services. The reason for this shift in policy is that its affirmative action characteristics offended Conservatives, who preferred that every student in the province be treated "equally." The argument of society-wide discrimination against certain groups and the thesis that such communities required educated leaders, both of which had been contentions of the New Democrats, was overruled by the Conservatives' belief that many others in their own, often rural, communities had had to overcome similar disadvantages.

It is probably worth noting that affirmative action has been at the centre of many debates in the United States. Indeed, the Toronto *Globe and Mail*, in an editorial on the visible minority report of the 1996 census, suggested that affirmative action was

> a very American idea, driven by a very American circumstance: 400 years of poisoned relations between blacks and whites, 300 years of slavery garnished with 100 years of Jim Crow . . . That is not our history and, more to the point, it isn't Canada today. Who we are today matters, because more than 70 percent of visible-minority Canadians were born outside Canada. Our future may be together, but our past was not. And together, we have the opportunity to make a new start and build a multiracial, non-racialist society.[5]

These are noble thoughts, of course, and desirable goals. But are they historically accurate? The experience of western Canada and of aboriginal Canadians suggests, rather, that conflicts between racial and ethnic groups are deeply rooted in Canadian experience. The issue is not whether Canada has ever been afflicted by racial prejudice—it has—but whether such government programs work to inject greater fairness into the job market, to establish a leadership cadre committed to socially responsible action and, in the process, to encourage greater sensitivity in daily relations among people of different races and ethnicities. It is a debate about the meaning of "equality" and the relative priority of freedom and equality in community life.

I V

THE CIRCUMSTANCE OF ABORIGINAL Canadians offers a particular illustration of the difficulties of reconciling the demands of freedom and equality. In recent years aboriginal leaders have established a wide-ranging political agenda. Not surprisingly, western Canadians have responded to it in different ways. Still, one can say that westerners are more aware than many of their compatriots, no doubt because they confront such issues regularly, that it is necessary to inject a sense of urgency into these national political discussions.

What is striking about these discussions is that they must be understood not just in terms of two political voices, as two leading parties contend for power, but also in terms of a third powerful voice, that of the aboriginal people themselves. As the latter are quick to point out, they have exceptional historic claims unlike those of any other group in Canadian society. The existence of three factions in the debate over aboriginal policy naturally makes the position of the wider public more uncomfortable. Nonetheless, the awkwardness cannot be avoided because aboriginal people, as a consequence of the 1982 Constitution but also because of their unique history, are not like other Canadians.

Some Canadians have responded with sympathy to the aboriginal situation and a determination to right the wrongs of the past. Others have argued that it is time to move on and that only firm consistent rejections of special pleading, as they characterize the First Nations position, will suffice.

An example of those willing to recant the old policies is the Aboriginal Rights Coalition, a group initiated by Canada's churches. The coalition has encouraged the preparation of formal apologies to aboriginal peoples "confessing the churches' role in the destruction of aboriginal spirituality, culture, and language." It has also lobbied governments and corporations, arguing that the "problems facing aboriginal communities today—loss of land and culture, development on aboriginal lands without their consent, and the struggle for self-determination—are still rooted in the values and lifestyles of the non-aboriginal mainstream, including many church-goers." The coalition calls for a "new covenant" between aboriginal and non-aboriginal peoples that will "guarantee the rights and responsibilities of aboriginal peoples in Canada."[6]

The opposing position is more diverse. The Calgary political scientist, Thomas Flanagan, has argued that such groups as the coalition are "killing with kindness." He noted a number of deaths by violence on a reserve near Calgary, an aboriginal settlement where, he said, sixty percent of the 3,300 residents lived on social assistance despite large numbers of available jobs in the area surrounding them. His target was not the aboriginal people themselves, he said, but the social assistance payments and special programs on housing, education, medical care and tax exemptions for aboriginal people that "distorted" market forces and created "a museum of costly failures." Ultimately aboriginal people must enter the wider labour market, Flanagan suggested: "Flipping burgers, bagging groceries, waiting on tables—such entry-level jobs are the first rung on the ladder of self-sufficiency and self-respect....Will politicians ever change the incentive structure that leads too many Stoneys [Assiniboines] to remain idle in the midst of so much work?"[7] The debate will be familiar to all Canadians and, indeed, to citizens in other countries. This does not mean that its answers are obvious.

The aboriginal agenda varies with the province and the band, but its tendency is the same everywhere: first, aboriginal people have a right to expect respect from the rest of the community, to the point that no aboriginal person need endure racism as a normal part of life; second, aboriginal people require some kind of acknowledgment of sovereignty, an acknowledgment that will permit them to consider in their own assemblies a wide range of community concerns (note that the meaning of the term "sovereignty" is far from agreed on); third, aboriginal people demand a degree of shared control (with government and private interests) over certain resources and, more generally, insist upon aboriginal ownership of certain tracts of land; fourth, aboriginal people have a right to equal access (equal to that of other Canadians) to a minimum of such basic public services as education, health care, roads and landing strips.

What should western Canadians be pressing the nation to do? Moses Okimaw, lawyer for the Assembly of Manitoba Chiefs, replies that they should urge the rapid devolution of powers from Ottawa to local aboriginal bands. Okimaw supports some of the recommendations of the Royal Commission on Aboriginal People, which issued its landmark report in November 1996, but he goes much farther in insisting upon a renegotiation of the relations between Canada and the First Nations. He seeks aboriginal economic power, as well as aboriginal jurisdiction over lands and people. A former chief at God's River, Manitoba, Okimaw believes that only a new start in Canada–First Nations relations can provide the necessary foundation for equality. Native Canadians must be recognized as having sovereignty over matters of daily life. As he puts it, they must "throw off the yoke of colonialism" that has held them back for more than a century.[8]

Western Canadians, aboriginal and non-aboriginal, must respond to these challenges. Yet they have not been helped by their

government in Ottawa. In the national election of 1997, barely a
word about aboriginal affairs was uttered by the governing party, the
Liberals, or its leading opponent, the Reform Party.[9] There were
two newsworthy initiatives in the following year: a "Statement of
Reconciliation: Learning from the Past" issued by the federal government, and a private member's bill in the House of Commons to
pardon Louis Riel, Métis leader, for his part in the uprising of 1885.
These acts do not change the material circumstances of Canadian or
aboriginal Canadian life.[10]

Significant change in national aboriginal policy has been long in
coming. The federal statement of reconciliation, which is not a formal apology, stands alone at the present time. Dismantling of the
federal Department of Indian Affairs proceeds very slowly in the test
case, Manitoba, and has not won widespread support. Schools, local
government and fire protection now rest under band control, and
funds are transferred by Ottawa to the bands for these purposes. But
the central concerns, such as judicial institutions and economic policy, seem to have been eclipsed by daily events.

Native Canadians are themselves taking control of the agenda.
In each of the western universities, aboriginal students are grad-
uating from the various faculties and moving into positions of
authority within their communities. They are joining the pioneers
in demanding reviews of their status, their land claims and their
community's economic needs. Moses Okimaw was one of a small
but effective group at the University of Manitoba in the early 1970s
that included Elijah Harper, MLA and MP, Ovide Mercredi and Phil
Fontaine, both national chiefs of the Assembly of First Nations,
and Murray Sinclair, assistant chief judge of the provincial court in
Manitoba. This generation of leaders established significant beach-
heads within the larger community, winning respect and making
history as the first in their communities to undertake such political
and legal work. If they were relatively few in number in those years,
they are not any longer.[11]

Moreover, there seems to be a reservoir of goodwill in both aboriginal and non-aboriginal communities. The popularity of aboriginal cultural productions, from Tomson Highway's plays and Tom
Jackson's "Huron Carole" to the CBC's aboriginal drama, "North of
Sixty," is a measure of national interest. But it is a long way from
music and drama to the struggle for daily bread in the aboriginal districts of Winnipeg's north end. The goodwill must be translated into
effective responses to poverty and despair.

V

AFFIRMATIVE ACTION IS JUST one of a number of issues on which western Canadian debates about multiculturalism and aboriginal status have centred. Deeper and more foreboding as an expression of such issues is race hatred. A number of widely publicized incidents concerning hate literature, hate groups and racial violence have struck Canadians forcibly in recent years. Some of these have originated in western Canada.

The existence of racist groups in western Canada provides one illustration of the social dangers in any society. Another illustration was a 1998 schoolyard brawl in Calgary involving two different racial groups, a machete and a brutal beating. Yet others include the Holocaust denials offered by a former teacher to his high school classes in Alberta, the web site service offered to white supremacist groups by a British Columbia company, the public campaign against alterations in the RCMP uniform that accommodate differing customs regarding hair and dress, and the murder of a Sikh temple caretaker allegedly by five men motivated by racial hatred.[12] Every western province can offer examples of racial conflict to match these headlines.

Moreover, every community leader could respond to these moments as did the premier of British Columbia, Glen Clark, when asked about the murder at the Sikh temple: "Clearly if [the allegations] are true, we need to do more. It's a shocker for me and I'm sure for all British Columbians to see that this could happen in British Columbia. I just never would have thought that this kind of racism could exist in British Columbia."[13] These are the pressure points in a society that is changing rapidly. They represent failures of course, but they do not suggest that racism pervades an entire community. Nonetheless, incidents such as the murder of the Sikh temple caretaker or of the Native Canadian trapper in Prince Albert do affect our response to the world.

Affirmative action versus individual liberty: the phrase illustrates the ways in which western Canada's leaders have crystallized the political choices they wish to present to the citizenry. In general, the provincial New Democrats and federal Liberals stand on one side of this divide, the Reform Party and provincial Conservatives on the other. All Canadians will recognize the range of the debate and the necessity of making choices.

REFERENCES

1. Editorial, *Globe and Mail* 20 February 1998, A22.

2. Peter Clough, "It makes you wonder" Vancouver *Province* 5 April 1998, A4; John Colebourn, "Airport, cabbies to meet over protest" Vancouver *Province* 5 April 1998, A2; Robert Sarti, "Work hardships drive cabbie to protest" Vancouver *Sun* 4 April 1998.

3. Tom Flanagan, *Waiting for the Wave: The Reform Party and Preston Manning* (Toronto: Stoddart 1995) pp. 15, 215.

4. Patrick Basham, "The Beginning of the End for Affirmative Action?" *Fraser Forum* (December 1997) pp. 19–22.

5. Editorial, *Globe and Mail* 20 February 1998, A22.

6. Aboriginal Rights Coalition, "The Sacred Path: A Journey of Healing for Canadian Churches and Aboriginal Peoples" (Ottawa: nd ca 1995).

7. Tom Flanagan, "Killing with kindness" *Globe and Mail* 11 September 1997.

8. Moses Okimaw, "The Scope of Aboriginal Government Authority" paper delivered to conference on Royal Commission on Aboriginal People, McGill Institute for the Study of Canada, 1 February 1997.

9. John Gray, "Not a word about natives" *Globe and Mail* 24 May 1997, D1, 9.

10. The Statement of Reconciliation, part of "Gathering Strength —Canada's Aboriginal Action Plan," was issued on 7 January 1998 [text in *Winnipeg Free Press* 14 January 1998, A11; government advertisement in *Globe and Mail* 25 March 1998, A15]. The Riel issue is discussed by Desmond Morton, "Fantasy vs Riel-ity" *Montreal Gazette* 26 January 1998, B3.

11. Gail Marchessault, "Aboriginal graduation powwow history in making: Achievement well worth noting" *Winnipeg Free Press* 23 June 1998, A11.

12. Ross Howard, "Notorious Internet service closes" *Globe and Mail* 28 April 1998; and Howard, "Watchdog group eyes Vancouver band of bigots" and "Racism's victims taking a stand" *Globe and Mail* 23 April 1998, A8; Donald Campbell, "Immigration weighs on teens" *Winnipeg Free Press* 4 March 1998, A11; Doug Saunders, "Postcard from a hate-filled past" *Globe and Mail* 28 March 1998, C2.

13. Ross Howard, "Allegation killing was linked to race fuels talk of intolerance in B.C." *Globe and Mail* 23 April 1998, A8.

CHAPTER TWELVE

Debating the Family, Sexuality and Civil Relations

JUST AS THERE ARE SEVERAL publicly approved ways to debate the reception of immigrants and reconstruct western Canada's relations with aboriginal people, so there are several ways to debate sexuality, the family, the disabled and other such issues associated with civil society. Again, it is possible to distinguish a left and a right in these questions.

A letter to a newspaper commenting on Canada's collective loss of table manners and gracious speech offers an outline of the issues:

> Yes, people in the past appeared to have better table manners and more gracious speech, but...
>
> Forty-five years ago, when I started school, the hemophiliac boy down the street watched us from his front window. He couldn't walk, so naturally he couldn't go to school.
>
> Forty years ago, teachers slapped children across the face, publicly humiliated them and hit them with books, rulers and leather straps....
>
> Thirty-five years ago, at the provincial institution where I worked, some mentally handicapped children wore straitjackets 16 hours a day. It was not uncommon on Sunday afternoons for families from town to take a leisurely drive through the grounds to stare at any of the "freaks" who might have been outside. At this same institution, male

staff members were paid 15 percent more than the female staff members for identical work. We were told that this was because "men don't like this kind of work, so we have to encourage them."

Twenty-five years ago, the local New Year's Baby was declared ineligible for the traditional prizes because his mother was an unmarried woman. The sponsors clarified that the prizes were meant for the first legitimate baby born in 1973.

Yes, good table manners are pleasant, but they are just icing. They are no substitute for our dawning recognition that all human beings have dignity and deserve equal opportunities. Our country is just beginning to be civil.

Most Canadians would endorse the sentiments in this intelligent letter and praise its author for the clarity of her vision, though there might be one or two items on her list of gains to which they took exception. Consider the letter juxtaposed with it on the newspaper's correspondence page, commenting on any such notion that times are better today. This second writer emphasized

the level of respect with which people treated one another a few decades back. When I started work 40 years ago, I called my boss Mr.... [and] children had respect for their teachers and typically wore uniforms to school, rather than designer clothes for which they might be beaten up and robbed by some of today's little darlings. Men went to work, every day, in suits and ties. . . . I'm probably whistling Dixie, but I hope in my remaining years to see a return (backlash?) to the old order: kids taking apples (rather than guns) to school, and their teachers—backed up by parental concern at home—having the authority to resume teaching "respect" as a worthwhile virtue.[1]

Again, there is much in this letter, even though it contradicts the direction of the first, that many Canadians, particularly older Canadians, would endorse.

How does a society come to terms with these issues? The two letters seem to raise a long and diverse list of subjects. They comment on matters associated with gender, age, the family, discipline, civility, respect for elders, treatment of the ill and equality. Yet, the subjects raised do seem to have something in common.

Indeed, the American philosopher, Richard Rorty, suggests that they belong in a single category: how people treat each other. The view that is sharply critical of flexibility in judgments about other people and seeks a return to a simpler world where standards are firm and perhaps even attached to an eternal guide, he calls "sadism;" its opposite, the view that is generous in its judgments and ready to change standards, he describes as permitting "otherness" (race, sexual preference, alternative families) to be socially acceptable.[2]

A conservative, such as Allan Bloom or Tom Flanagan or David Frum, might approach this same discussion by applying the disapproving label "politically correct" to those who shift the standards of acceptability to include the formerly deviant. They might not object, however, to grouping all these issues in a single category. Preston Manning's Reform Party, indeed, describes these subjects as belonging under the rubric of "social conservatism."

The writer of the first letter, who happens to live in Surrey, British Columbia, believes that things have changed for the better in the past generation. The writer of the second letter, the one whistling Dixie, believes, like many conservatives, that things have become worse. The two positions divide left from right on matters of civil relations, family and the household.

I

CIVIL RELATIONS HAVE BEEN the subject of many recent debates in western Canada. One of the most common concerns the place of gay and lesbian people in the community. Many of these contests occur in relation to the school system. The Surrey, British Columbia, school board, for example, banned three children's books on the grounds that they depicted same-sex families. The decision was challenged in court by two gay teachers, a Surrey parent and a student, whose lawyer argued that the values represented in the books were laudable, and that to ban the books was to give preferential treatment to the religious views of certain parents. Similarly, a debate arose in Winnipeg over a teacher's request that she be permitted to reveal her lesbianism to her class. An opponent, who wrote that tolerance in Canada "has come to mean the imposition of undesirable political and social agendas upon the masses by those who hold power," argued that his own Christian views were too often dismissed: "A simple and brief examination of how the public and media are allowed to ridicule Christians, and Christian beliefs, with impunity is just one indication of our schizophrenic condition. Our lack of logic in regards to 'tolerance' is unparalleled."[3]

As these examples suggest, such debates can carry the issue into quite unexpected terrain. In British Columbia, the NDP government became the first in Canada to pass legislation giving "gay and lesbian couples the same privileges as heterosexuals for child support, custody and access." It also passed legislation declaring explicitly that same-sex couples have the same right to pension benefits within public sector jobs as heterosexual couples. The expected response came from those opposed to such changes in the definition of family. Thus, former premier William Vander Zalm, newly named president of the B.C. Reform Party, said: "I believe in the traditional family, as does the Reform Party."

The 1994 Ottawa assembly of the Reform Party spoke directly to this issue. Its resolution read: "Resolved that the Reform Party support limiting the definition of a legal marriage as the union of a woman and a man, and that this definition be used in the provision of spousal benefits for any program funded or administered by the federal government."[4]

The Roman Catholic Archbishop of Vancouver introduced a new consideration into the discussion, however, by suggesting that the pension benefits should be available to a wide range of loved ones, not just heterosexual and homosexual partners. Archbishop Exner's intervention implied that "fair" legislation would recognize many stable family relationships, such as unmarried siblings, lifelong friends and children who care for aging parents. His suggestion placed a much wider definition of the family at the centre of debate. As Exner said, "If you extend pension benefits only to homosexual couples, you are in fact giving them the same treatment you are giving to families. That, I think, diminishes the family. It kind of erodes and undermines the special role of family in society." As in discussion of the B.C. legislation, Exner could expect support from "evangelical Christian, Sikh, Muslim and Hindu leaders." He could expect opposition, reported the *Vancouver Sun*, from the Anglican and United churches.[5] And though the newspaper did not mention it, he would find political support on one side of the political spectrum, not on the other. Once again, liberal and conservative views on definitions of public civility confronted each other. Yet Exner's analysis was actually much more complicated than this single left-right dualism was able to express.

An Alberta case, in which Delwin Vriend was fired from an Edmonton Christian school because he was gay, has sparked the clearest political divisions in western Canada. Vriend could not file a human rights complaint in Alberta because its human rights legislation omitted mention of gays and lesbians. Vriend appealed to the Supreme Court of Canada on the grounds that he should have been entitled to human rights protection. The Supreme Court decided in his favour and added sexual orientation to the list of types of discrimination prohibited in the province.

Two different types of response could be discerned in the storm of controversy that followed. First, the conventional debate pitted defenders of gays and lesbians against those who opposed this orientation. A conservative caller to a radio show said the Supreme Court ruling "opens the doors for forcing churches and institutions like King's College [Vriend's former employer] to keep that person on in a position which totally goes against the teachings of the faith." This view was reinforced by a Calgary professor of political science who argued that the only minorities now being protected were those "favoured by the social left. Why not unborn children, why not smokers, why not gun owners? . . . There's a political bias. This minorities game can be played left, right and centre and the court plays it right down the left lane."[6]

A second and increasingly important contention emerged in the weeks following the Vriend ruling. It held that the Supreme Court was the problem, not gay and lesbian rights alone. This debate challenged the ruling not on religious or philosophical or sexual grounds, but rather, on the grounds that judges, who were presuming to define the character of the family, should not have such power.

This second issue produced more complications for those who seek a political road map through modern society. In general, Liberals and New Democrats and the Supreme Court itself stood on one side, and the Reform Party and Conservatives on the other. But metropolitan centres were more open to change than were rural communities; so were British Columbians more than Saskatchewanians, the young more than the old, whatever the partisan loyalties in other matters. Thus the debates within each party were often as intense as those between parties.

In the Supreme Court ruling on the Vriend case, Justice Frank
Iacobucci declared that the 1982 Charter of Rights created "a new
social contract that was democratically chosen" by Canada's parliamentary representatives "as part of a redefinition of our democracy." Henceforth, "the legislatures and executive must perform
their roles in conformity with the newly conferred constitutional
rights and freedoms. That the courts were the trustees of these
rights insofar as disputes arose concerning their interpretation was
a necessary part of this new design." A new "dialogue" had opened
between legislatures and courts, he suggested, and the result was
an enhancement of the democratic process.[7] This has been the
position represented by Liberal and New Democrat defenders of
the court.

The Reform Party and some Alberta Conservatives have rejected
the court's interventions, as they see it, into spheres reserved for
family, church and government. They oppose, as the *Edmonton Sun*
put it, the "secular high priests" of the Supreme Court imposing
their views upon Alberta legislators. In his statement on "judicial
activism," Preston Manning proposed that a judicial review committee be created by the House of Commons to "ensure the
supremacy of the elected representatives of the people of Canada
and the accountability of the judiciary."[8]

The conservative columnist Gordon Gibson also criticized this
use of judicial powers. In terms reminiscent of Terry Morley's challenge to the Delgamuukw ruling, Gibson addressed the Supreme
Court's revision of Alberta law in the Vriend case: "Forcing the
change by the fiat of what amounts to a foreign court is much less
satisfactory for all concerned than arriving at the same result
through the political process."[9] Like Morley's dyspeptic comments,
this condemnation challenged the legitimacy of a fundamental
Canadian institution.

The range of the civility debates is extraordinary. They
involve not only gays and lesbians but common-law marriages,
divorce, disability, abortion, child-care support for one-parent
families, the exercise of male authority in marriage relationships
and of parental authority over children, tax law as it relates to
dependents (spouses, children and others) who do not have paid
employment, medical decisions such as do-not-resuscitate orders
and many others. There is no consistent rule to determine who
will choose which side—the alleged conservative or the erstwhile
liberal.

At the heart of such discussions, increasingly, are concerns about the family. In the 1960s, ninety percent of children were "born to mothers and fathers who were married for the first time and who had never lived as a couple, either together or with others, prior to marriage." In 1993-94 twenty percent of all births occurred in common-law families and nearly two-thirds of such children, by the age of twelve, watched the breakup of the parental relationship, over four times as many as those born into married families.[10]

Such issues now shape political fortunes and are raising significant public policy questions. If the reactions of ordinary Canadians seem to fall into no apparent patterns, Western Canada's parties nonetheless divide along the expected liberal–conservative axis. Reform and traditional Conservative activists lean to the view that there is a fixed human nature. They often contend that a body of unchanging principles guides family life. Those on the other side of the spectrum are not necessarily relativists—that is, they do not necessarily argue that all beliefs are equally valid—but they are more willing to accept differences, change standards and seek a new consensus.

An illustration of the liberal perspective is a recent approach to household issues introduced by the social democratic government in Saskatchewan.[11] A Labour Department discussion paper on the problems facing families and individuals defined the issue not as one of ideal family roles, but of a particular contemporary reality—the increasing proportion of all parents who are working for wages. The discussion document presented statistics on women's work to demonstrate that two-thirds of women with preschool children had jobs outside the home. A similar proportion of families depended on two incomes. One-third of farm operators, both male and female, had off-farm jobs. The document asserted that time-stress, due to a shortage of day care facilities, the inflexibility of employment rules and the demands of the home (employed women spend twice as much time on unpaid household work as their male counterparts, according to the study document) put intolerable burdens on individuals and removed essential supports from the community. The goal of the planning exercise was to alleviate the stress of "our 'hurried' culture" and to find means of "creating more harmony between work and family."

The NDP government's solutions, insofar as they were evident in this impeccably democratic process, did not lie in recovering the gender roles of previous generations but in revised work rules, flex time, leaves and sabbaticals. In other words, the social democratic government of Saskatchewan, like its northern European counterparts, would find means of alleviating stress by revising labour law to address workers' concerns.

In contrast, when the Conservative government of Manitoba in the same period revised labour laws, its concern was to strengthen management rights and to reduce the allegedly sweeping powers of union leaders. The family issues addressed in the Saskatchewan document were left to individual Manitobans to resolve. When Manitoba Conservatives did respond to the same household pressures, their concern was to strengthen the traditional family unit by increasing, for example, the support allocated to private educational institutions (as opposed to public schools), which taught the appropriate family values.

The lesson implicit in a survey of household, family and civil relations is that similar social concerns can be addressed by very different types of analysis and policy. Western Canada's version of the international debate is waged with Conservatives and Reformers on one side, and the Social Democrats and Liberals on the other.

REFERENCES

1. Both letters appeared in the *Globe and Mail*, 3 June 1998, A27. The first was by Carolyn Germain Smith, Surrey B.C., and the second by Dave Ashby, Peterborough, Ontario.

2. Richard Rorty, *Achieving Our Country: Leftist Thought in Twentieth Century America* (Cambridge: Harvard University Press 1998), and "The American road to fascism" *New Statesman* 8 May 1998, p. 28–9; I would like to thank Bill Brooks for this reference.

3. The debate occurred in *The Metro* (Winnipeg), 5 and 12 August 1998. The author cited is Donald Richmond. He was replying to columnist Donald Benham.

4. Tom Flanagan, *Waiting for the Wave: The Reform Party and Preston Manning* (Toronto: Stoddart 1995) p. 197.

5. Douglas Todd, "Gay sex, politics and religion are explosive mix" *Vancouver Sun* 11 July 1998, A1, 10; Robert Matas, "B.C. expands same-sex rights" *Globe and Mail* 23 June 1998, A1, 9.

6. *Vancouver Sun*, "Critics of Supreme Court say it has a leftist bias" and "Gay rights ruling leaves Alberta divided" 3, 4 April 1998.

7. These quotations from the decision were cited in *Vancouver Sun*, "Critics of Supreme Court say it has a leftist bias" 3 April 1998, A10.

8. *Edmonton Sun* quotation cited in *Vancouver Sun*, 3 April 1998, A10; Preston Manning, "Parliament, not judges, must make the laws of the land" *Globe and Mail* 16 June 1998, A23.

9. Gordon Gibson, "Good fences would make good judges" *Globe and Mail* 14 April 1998, A23. Gibson defended the outrageous phrase, "foreign court," by saying: "Neither the people nor legislature of Alberta has any say whatsoever in the composition or mandate of the Supreme Court of Canada. That the current federal Justice minister is an Albertan is both transient and means nothing. Appointment of the Supremes is the sole prerogative of the prime minister. Interestingly, the Alberta

Court of Appeal—still appointed by the feds but at least composed of Albertans resident in the province—did find the
Vriend issue to be one for the legislature, not the courts."

10. Nicole Marcil-Gratton in a report for Statistics Canada, cited in
Jane Gadd, "Out-of-wedlock births increasing" *Globe and Mail*
13 August 1998, A5; and *Calgary Herald*, "Core Values: Divorce
stats show children pay the price" 12 June 1998, A14.

11. The NDP Labour Department, typically, released a working
paper for discussion, "Balancing Work and Family," followed by
community hearings and an academic research study. Then, a
commission report was published and presented to a provincial
conference on the topic. Out of this planning and education
initiative would come the momentum for new policies. The
momentum would encompass community awareness, interest
group commitment to making changes, and union and management involvement, as well as legislation, if that was deemed
necessary.

CHAPTER THIRTEEN

The Market
vs. the Government

INDIVIDUALS SHOULD BE FREE TO seek their own destiny, be responsible for the efforts they make towards that end and not be hampered by red tape, bureaucracy or excessive taxes. Who could disagree?

Individuals should be equal before the courts, at the ballot box and in their access to educational institutions and health-care facilities. Again, who could disagree?

Yet these two principles, freedom and equality, are often said to be in conflict in the community.[1] Indeed, support for one and criticism of the other establishes a clear political fault line in contemporary western Canada.

I

HOW MUCH RELIANCE SHOULD one place on governmental and market institutions in the organization of community life? As a result of campaigns by conservatives during the past twenty years, government spending—the role of the public sector—has become a central issue in western Canadian politics. Discussion of budget deficits, balanced budget amendments and taxes separates social democrats from conservatives every time, whether in Saskatchewan coffee shops or in British Columbia party battles.

A much-publicized symbol of this debate is "tax freedom" day, which, in 1998, occurred on June 26. The idea was popularized by the Fraser Institute, a publicity agency grafted onto a research office, which introduced it in 1977 as a means of illustrating the role of government in Canadians' lives. It establishes the proportion of the year required to "pay the total tax bill imposed on [Canadians] by all levels of government." According to the authors of the 1998 press release, on this day "Canadians finally start working for themselves." Before this date, they were paying for three levels of government. The Fraser Institute wants to establish "the impact of the most complex and intrusive activity of government—its tax-collecting apparatus."[2]

The concept is based on the sensible principle that all the money earned by a worker belongs to the worker. In this sense, like every other citizen in society, including the most wealthy and powerful, this worker, too, possesses private property—the wages accrued in exchange for labour.

Implicit in this message are ideas that travel in two directions. The first is a democratic and collective notion: the worker pays taxes voluntarily, agrees on public levies to meet public priorities and supervises tax levels indirectly by means of participation in political discussions and, ultimately, at the ballot box.

The second is individualist: the property in question (the wage relinquished in a tax payment) is indeed private. It is being taken from you for purposes about which you have only a vague understanding and which are often bogus. You alone know how it can best be spent. And if you were free to allocate it in accordance with market mechanisms, you would contribute to the most efficient use of society's resources while taking responsibility for your own choices. Implicitly we are being told by the "tax freedom" message that the government will not spend efficiently or in ways that benefit you.

The Fraser Institute, with its headquarters in Vancouver, is just one of a half-dozen agencies located in western Canada that attempt to influence public opinion "by espousing smaller government and more reliance on competitive markets."[3] The other five include the *Alberta Report* magazine group (Edmonton), the Canadian Taxpayers Federation (Regina), the Canada West Foundation, the Reform Party and the National Citizens' Coalition (Calgary). All are dedicated to promoting conservative ideas. As the Fraser Institute's executive director, Michael Walker, has said, "If you really want to change the world, you have to change the ideological fabric of the world."[4]

The Fraser Institute employs between twenty and thirty staff on its annual budget of nearly $3 million. It claims to be the "largest privately funded, public policy research organization in Canada." Its mandate is "the redirection of public attention to the role of

competitive markets in providing for the well-being of Canadians."
It publishes articles, books and press releases, and it organizes an
extensive series of student meetings on university campuses. It
describes its publications and seminars as "'products'. . . where we
took the initiative to create a public policy event." The funding for
the institute comes from corporate donations.

The chairman of the Fraser Institute board, R.J. Addington,
illustrated the tenor of its work with his comments on the completion of an institute project, *Economic Freedom of the World:
1975–1995*, by James Gwartney, Robert Lawson and Walter Block.
Quoting his colleague, Michael Walker, Addington noted that

> most financial transactions, including contributions
> to political parties and other completely private
> affairs, now require that the social insurance num-
> ber of the citizen be reported so that the transaction
> can be traced. The essential point is that there is a
> very close connection between economic freedom
> and political freedom, and if individuals don't have
> economic freedom, then it is very difficult for them
> to exercise meaningful political freedom. . . .
>
> The Institute's ambition in producing the Eco-
> nomic Freedom Index is nothing short of changing
> the nature of public discourse about the role of
> government in society. It is our ambition, by creat-
> ing an international measurement movement, to
> ensure that adequate attention is paid to the impli-
> cations of government actions for the level of eco-
> nomic freedom. Economic freedom is the most
> basic freedom that people require.[5]

The notion of economic freedom is founded on the thesis that
consumer control in anonymous marketplace transactions contributes to the efficient functioning of the community and to the social
maturity of the individual. Proponents of greater freedom argue that
government decisions, which are inevitably in the hands of blind
fools known as "planners," or worse, "central planners," create chaos
(see, for proof, the collapse of the Soviet Union's planned economy
in the 1980s), whereas restructuring in private sector industries constitutes "relatively painless change."[6]

The big targets of this conservative campaign at the turn of the
twenty-first century are health care and education. A $75 billion

industry in Canada, nationalized and therefore untouched by the magic of the market's invisible hand, health care is the subject of intense debate. Education is a target of even greater importance because it is still often beyond the market's reach and is said to inculcate beliefs that undermine the extension of market principles. Milton Friedman, the economist whose work stands at the foundation of the Fraser Institute, has placed great emphasis on the improvement of the educational system in North America as a prerequisite for further economic growth. By this means, he says, lower-skilled workers can become higher-skilled workers. What stands in the way of this desirable transition is "the incompetence of the increasingly decrepit U.S. public school monopoly." Friedman argued in a speech to the Fraser Institute:

> [T]he way to do something about our educational
> system is to privatize it, to enable the forces of pri-
> vate enterprise, which are so innovative and pro-
> gressive, to reshape the educational system in a way
> that will reduce greatly the fraction of the popula-
> tion that's in these low-skilled areas.[7]

Shortly thereafter, the Fraser Institute resolved to make educational issues one focus of its work.[8]

Where does the social democrat take issue with the proponent of markets? One of the central issues in this debate is why growth takes place in an economy. Where Friedman praises the efficiency of markets and the power of technological change, his opponents speak of "post-neoclassical endogenous growth theory." Aside from the mouthful of syllables, the left is saying that some types of investment produce far more economic growth than others, and that investments by government in infrastructure—better transportation and health facilities, better education, better science research—are more effective than the influences (technical change, population growth) praised by the free market enthusiasts. Thus, the social democrat believes in the public sector, seeks its modernization and promotes its efficiency.[9] Far from scorning planning, the social democrat—witness the Saskatchewan examples concerning highway reconstruction and family stress cited above—emphasizes it.

Who is winning and losing in these battles? University of Calgary political scientist Tom Flanagan would have you believe that the conservative public relations institutes have won the war. He claims:

> [T]he West has learned how to fight back. Its
> research institutes and political movements pro-
> duce the ideas that dominate today's political
> agenda. The results are evident in the two biggest
> issues of all: fiscal policy and national unity. Bal-
> anced budgets are now conventional wisdom. Tax
> cuts are coming. The role of the state in relation to
> civil society is shrinking as government programs
> are downsized, redesigned and privatized.[10]

This is historical nonsense. Balanced budgets did not come
from the Fraser Institute and groups of that ilk. The Saskatchewan
CCF and NDP governments ran one small deficit and thirty surpluses
in their thirty-one years in power between 1944 and 1982. The
highest priority in the Romanow government, after it returned to
power in 1991, was to get Saskatchewan's books back into the black
after a decade of Conservative deficits. In the era when many Canadian governments did let budgets get out of control, from the late
1970s to the early 1990s, the Manitoba NDP government was the
first to turn the tide by revising spending patterns and tax levels. In
1988, the year it fell from power, the province produced a surplus.

Despite Flanagan's expression of certainty about rollbacks in
public spending, both the Manitoba and Saskatchewan social democratic parties, like that in British Columbia, support policy planning
and the public sector as necessary instruments in the government of
small peripheral societies such as the provinces of the Canadian
West. The British journalist William Keegan, speaking from the
other side of the fence to Flanagan, offered his expression of relief
about the passing of Thatcherism that, in its sense of finality,
sounds very like Flanagan's expression of delight about the passing
of social democracy. In his comments on the British Labour Party's
1998–2001 spending plans, Keegan reported: "At least no one is now
arguing that the appropriate ratio of public spending to gross
domestic product is twenty-five percent, rather than forty percent."[11]
Needless to say, Canada's right has also talked of the twenty-five
percent target, and the left has defended the forty percent ratio. To
both left and right, and to Flanagan and Keegan, I would say that the
battle is not over and it will not end anytime soon.

The West's ongoing bickering about the Canadian Wheat
Board illustrates the continuing contest between conservative and
social democrat. The board, based in Winnipeg, receives wheat and

barley from Canadian farmers and acts as the exclusive seller of this grain in the export market, as it has done for half a century. The prices fluctuate over the year, of course, depending on the thousand global factors that affect the growing of foods, and the board nego- tiates many sales contracts. Having tided over the farm family with an initial payment upon receipt of its grain, the board calculates interim and final payments based on the average selling price for the entire year for grain of each type and quality. The producer gets no special advantage for having delivered at one time or one elevator rather than another but, equally, loses nothing by having chosen to deliver when markets were glutted or by owning a farm situated many hundreds of miles from the export terminus.

The Wheat Board is, no mistake about it, a government-run business. It may be an independent entity, operating at arm's length from the cabinet, but its monopoly is guaranteed by legislation and its structure is established by Parliament. A private enterprise cor- poration it is not.

The Wheat Board is anathema to those who like to take their markets raw. Alberta columnists David Bercuson and Barry Cooper describe its powers as a "tyranny" held by "a nanny government." They attribute the board's continued existence to the inevitable desire of governments to possess greater power: "There is only one reason for its continuing monopoly. Food is even more important to humanity than uranium [which is also controlled by a government monopoly, the Atomic Energy Control Board], while the ability to influence the global trade in grain is a tremendous potential source of power and influence to any government." Therein lies the source of conservative opposition: the power over the grain trade is held in the hands of political representatives rather than the marketplace.[12]

Those who are willing to trade a chance of greater gain—or loss—for greater security believe that the might of a corporation occupying over one-fifth of the world market for wheat and barley, and the advantage of receiving an averaged annual price, outweighs the thrill of the gamble, the uncertain prospect of a gain and the satisfaction of assuming greater responsibility for the farm house- hold's survival.

Alberta barley growers, who are located closer to American brewers eager to bid on their malting barley, tend to oppose the Wheat Board monopoly. Northern Saskatchewan and Manitoba wheat growers, who are located far from the export terminals and, who perhaps feel less certain about anyone's ability to anticipate

trends in international markets, tend to support the board. Then
there are those between the two poles who are ambivalent in their
sentiments. Taken as a whole, the small to medium-size farms spe-
cializing to some degree in wheat constitute a strong majority in
favour of the monopoly ("single-desk") selling agency. As the Manitoba Pool told a government investigation into the board's operations, the advantage of Canada's assurance of grain quality and the
gains in price outweighed all other arguments in the debate.[13]

The same type of debate has occurred over Crown corporations
in the western provinces. In Manitoba, for example, the Conservative government sold off the Manitoba Telephone System (MTS) in
1996, arguing that changing circumstances in global telecommuni-
cations required the leanness, flexibility and decisiveness that could
be provided only by private sector managers responding to signals
from customers and shareholders in the marketplace.

Next door in Saskatchewan, now governed by New Democrats,
a similar debate arose concerning Crown corporations such as the
telephone, power and bus monopolies. However, the social democratic administration has not seen fit to sell off its holdings. Rather,
it has participated in a debate about how these giant corporations
can best serve the people. This debate, following the lead of the
management professor Henry Mintzberg, distinguishes not two but
four types of ownership: private and state ownership of course, but
also "co-operatively owned" and "non-owned," the latter including
not-for-profit organizations such as hospitals, universities and voluntary agencies. Mintzberg suggests that the first two, despite their
apparent differences, are really quite similar because they are tightly
controlled through hierarchies, whether by private owners or the
state. The only big contrast lies in the destination of the profits, the
former to shareholders, the latter to the government. The importance of the second two is that they contribute to "a balanced economy." Indeed, according to Mintzberg, all four types of
organization work together to make distinctive contributions and to
perform specific functions that the others might not perform as
well, if at all.

The Saskatchewan debate, and the awareness of the different
types and roles of economic organizations, have raised the broader
question of why Crown corporations exist. They began because
only the government could sustain the great uneconomic public
crusades needed to deliver important kinds of community-building
infrastructure such as telephone service and electricity to scattered

hamlets and farmsteads. They continued because they permitted cross-subsidization, which is the practice of levying differential fees that ensures a basic minimum service at minimum cost to every subscriber.

Today, according to Brett Fairbairn, professor of Co-operative Studies at the University of Saskatchewan, the giant state-owned monopolies offer fewer distinct advantages over private corporations unless they learn the sophisticated lessons taught by co-operatives. They must study the co-ops' experience with the role and membership of boards of directors, the co-ops' expertise in conducting conversations with dispersed constituencies and the co-op's ability to define social missions for a business enterprise. The purpose of such study is to redefine the relations between corporation and community by focusing on "the social and economic health of the communities they serve." In other words, unlike the private corporation that must serve the narrowly defined financial interests of the shareholder (often an absentee landlord whose interest is the balance sheet, not the community), the reconstructed Crown corporation must be dedicated to "community economic development."[14] This is a quite different view of a business's governance and purpose.

Like the right, the left in western Canada is reconsidering economic institutions that have played a central role in economic life for several generations. They are utilizing labour-sponsored investment funds and community-elected boards of credit unions to redirect economic development. They have established think tanks, such as the Canadian Centre for Policy Alternatives (Manitoba branch) and the Parklands Institute (Edmonton), in response to the success of the conservative organizations. The debate goes on.

REFERENCES

1. William L. Miller, Annis May Timpson and Michael Lessnoff, *Political Culture in Contemporary Britain: People and Politicians, Principles and Practice* (Oxford: Clarendon Press 1996).

2. Joel Emes and Michael Walker, "At Last, an Earlier Tax Freedom Day in 1998" *Fraser Forum* July 1998, p. 10. A critical survey of the impact of institutes of the Fraser type is Richard Crockett's *Thinking the Unthinkable: Think-Tanks and the Economic Counter-Revolution, 1931–1983* (London: HarperCollins, 1995)

3. Tom Flanagan, "The political power of the West" *Globe and Mail* 26 February 1998, A21.

4. Frances Russell, "Fraser Institute's agenda" *Winnipeg Free Press* 20 March 1998.

5. The above two paragraphs are based on the Fraser Institute's *1996 Annual Report*, 1–3. I would like to thank Laura Jones, environmental economist, for kindly giving me a tour and outlining the work of the institute.

6. Terence Corcoran, "If markets drove health care" *Winnipeg Free Press* 11 March 1997, B2. His article illustrates one of the recent subjects of North American debate, the application of market principles to medical institutions. The Fraser Institute also participates in these discussions.

7. Milton Friedman, "The Second Industrial Revolution" a speech to the Fraser Institute's 20th Anniversary Annual General Meeting, *Fraser Forum* September 1994 pp. 7–17. The Charter schools movement is the offspring of this perspective.

8. Dave Barrett, "Research, or hidden agenda?" *Globe and Mail* 20 March 1998, A21.

9. William Keegan, "Iron Chancellor melts Labour hearts" and Will Hutton, "Labour is moving in the right direction . . . " *The Observer* (London) 19 July 1998, B2, 30.

10. Flanagan, "The political power of the West" *Globe and Mail* 26 February 1998, A21.

11. Spending on programs by all governments in Canada (federal, provincial, municipal) peaked in 1992 at forty-seven percent of gross domestic product, and then fell to thirty-nine percent in 1997. It was about thirty percent in 1961; Bruce Little, "A trumpet blown a bit too hard" *Globe and Mail* 2 March 1998, A3.

12. Bercuson and Cooper adopt the posture of militant rebels in this column. Having declared that the "real issue" is "government power," they conclude: "Such an approach, against a background of growing dissatisfaction among Prairie producers, guarantees that the fight against the board will continue. There aren't enough jails in the nation to hold all the Dave Bryans [a farmer convicted of exporting grain without a permit] who want to control the fruits of their own labour." *Globe and Mail* 28 February 1998, D2; the newspaper's editorial board adopted the same position in its issue of 26 February 1998.

13. Manitoba Pool Elevators, "Submission to the Western Grain Marketing Panel" 23 February 1996, and Anders Bruun, "Alter the wheat board first" *Winnipeg Free Press* 28 January 1996, A7; Canadian Press, "Farmers win greater control over Canadian Wheat Board" *Calgary Herald* 12 June 1998, D13; Bud Robertson, "Wedge continues to be driven between farmers over the CWB" *Winnipeg Free Press* 25 March 1998, B5; Canadian Press, "Grain: Who should sell Canada's wheat" Montreal *Gazette* 10 April 1997, D7; Donald Campbell, "Alberta wages wheat war: Provincial government backs farmers against CWB" *Winnipeg Free Press* 9 August 1996, A11; Mathew Ingram, "Grain issues remain explosive" *Globe and Mail* 1 January 1998, B2.

14. Crown Investments Corporation of Saskatchewan, "Saskatchewan Crown Corporations Review 1996" and "Talking about Saskatchewan Crowns: A Report on the Public Review of the Future of Crown Corporations in Saskatchewan 1996"; the above discussion relies on Brett Fairbairn, "Balancing Act: Crown Corporations in a Successful Economy" (Saskatoon: University of Saskatchewan Centre for the Study of Co-operatives, June 1997), where the government documents are reviewed and linked to Henry Mintzberg, "Managing Government —Governing Management" *Harvard Business Review* May–June 1996, pp. 75–83.

CHAPTER FOURTEEN

Quebec, the Senate and the Future of Canada

CANADIANS SEEM TO HAVE AN unlimited tolerance for discussions about government. Not politics—every nation talks politics—but the actual institutions, powers and operations of government. Canadian jokes that have as a punch line "the elephant: federal or provincial responsibility" suggest a certain lack of excitement in daily life. Ah, Canadians—nice folks—don't get out much. Nevertheless, government institutions and the division of powers do seem to cause Canadian muscles to tauten and smiles to tighten. Beware when this happens, you visitors from elsewhere, because your seemingly harmless hosts are about to fly into a fit over federal–provincial relations. However, despite the peculiarities of these Canadians, I suggest that the flexibility of Canadian institutions and Canadians' understanding of the allocation of tasks among levels of government are virtues.

I

IT IS NO SURPRISE to hear that western Canadians, like citizens in every democracy, have expressed unhappiness with the alleged remoteness of their political representatives in recent years. Preston Manning of the Reform Party believes that this distrust of government and of political parties is a profound and widespread phenomenon that he can ride into the prime minister's office. Stephen Harper, former Reform MP and head of the National Citizens Coalition, a right-wing lobby group, has been quoted as saying that "one of the reasons interest groups are turning to populism or the courts is that our representative institutions aren't working."[1] Though similar statements have been made by many citizens in many countries, in Canada the issue has found the strongest response among populist parties of the right.

The Reform Party has undertaken its drive for power on the basis of four principles. Two of them, fiscal reform and social conservatism, have been discussed above. The other two, democratic accountability and reformed federalism, concern the very composition and powers of government institutions.[2]

Reform claims that it is a populist party, more responsive to ordinary citizens than the elite run traditional parties. In this, it is trying to stake out ground on the right parallel to that long held by the New Democrats, populists of the left.[3] Reform supports the introduction of a recall mechanism into electoral life, so that voters can remove by petition a representative who has lost favour. It also supports the use of referenda on important public policy issues. It claims, as do the New Democrats, to generate its policy from open discussion among ordinary Canadians—the grass roots, as all parties love to call them. It has challenged the role of the Supreme Court in relation to Parliament. It has called for cuts in government spending, of course, but also tax cuts, in order to reduce the very role of government in the community.[4]

Reform's most publicized policy stand in its early years, an expression of this populism, was its advocacy of a reformed Senate. Some westerners, following the political philosopher Friedrich von Hayek (whom a Fraser Institute employee identified as required reading at the institute), believe that a popularly elected second chamber in a parliamentary system could hamstring the parliamentary system and, thus, establish greater economic freedom for individuals and corporations. Others, perhaps less interested in such tactical analysis, and taking the American, German and Australian upper houses as precedents, believe that the principle of regional representation should be recognized more fully in the Canadian Constitution because Canada is a large and diverse federal state. Still others simply want their own way and blame outsiders—the East, Ontario, Bay Street, Quebec—for thwarting their political preferences. Reform contains examples of all three strains.

The objective of these revisionists is to change the mechanism of selecting Canada's upper chamber and to revise its powers. In this approach, senators would be elected. The Reform Party believes that an elected Senate would wield popular authority on Parliament

Hill comparable to that of the House of Commons. The number of representatives allocated to each of the constituent regions would be equal to that of every other region. Thus, Canada's geographic regions—whatever their population—would have as much power in one chamber as the most populous parts of the country now have in the other. After all, these Reformers argue, the principle of representation by population should be no more sacrosanct than representation by community. Moreover, the upper house should be permitted to exercise real legislative powers. Elected, equal, effective: these are the principles enshrined in the "western" campaign—which is really only a western conservative campaign—for a Triple-E Senate.

The reason behind the Triple-E campaign is not hard to find. Very few Canadians can muster much enthusiasm for a house appointed exclusively by the prime minister and in which the members sit until they reach seventy-five. In a speech to the House of Commons, Preston Manning said:

> The seven deadly sins of the current institution are fraudulent beginnings, compromised principles, partisan patronage of the worst kind, unethical conduct and work habits, abuse of privileges, a higher priority to partisan political work than to public service, and excessive costs in relation to negligible benefits.[5]

Left-wing populists from Tommy Douglas to Alexa McDonough have endorsed a similar view.

It is one thing to agree on the relatively unsatisfactory circumstances of the present Senate but quite another to find an acceptable alternative. New Democrats have argued for decades that the upper house should simply be abolished. In the past Liberals and Conservatives, who could always hope for their own translation to this better place, generally supported its continued existence. The Reform Party has, from its inception, favoured a Triple-E Senate. Interestingly, abolition of the second chamber has recently won support from a number of western Canadian commentators. Others remain convinced, however, for one or more of the reasons noted above, that the election of a few senators might initiate a larger movement to create a powerful and useful second chamber.[6]

The campaign to keep the Triple-E movement alive has been led by the Canada West Foundation of Calgary. This small agency,

which has a staff of about half a dozen and an annual budget of
$700,000 to $800,000, celebrated its twenty-fifth anniversary in
1997. Funded by business donors, in particular the families of two
wealthy Alberta families, F.C. Mannix ($500,000) and A.J.E. Child
($1 million), as well as earlier support from James Richardson
(Winnipeg) and G.M. Bell (Calgary), the foundation has produced
dozens of attractive pieces of literature on the western Canadian
economy, government deficits, free trade with the United States and
the Canadian constitutional debates.

The publications and conferences of the Canada West Foundation are not contributions to scholarship, but rather, brief, clear,
effectively designed works of advocacy. Growing out of the foundation's roots in the Calgary business community, its publications
program tends to combine support for corporate interests with a
vague "western-ness" that claims to speak for all of western Canada.
The foundation's greatest success was the moment when Premier
Klein adopted its plan to elect senators-in-waiting, choosing the
regular Alberta municipal elections of October 1998 as the vehicle
for a campaign.[7]

Hidden within this Alberta initiative on the Senate is another
principle of even greater potential significance. When Canada's premiers met to discuss a response to the Quebec referendum result of
1995, they approved the "Calgary Declaration," also known as "A
Framework for Discussion on Canadian Unity." Inevitably they
struggled with the dilemma of reconciling Canadians' aspirations to
live as equals while maintaining elements of diversity within the
community.

The Calgary principles contain expressions of both equality and
diversity. Of relevance to the discussion of the Triple-E Senate, they
include one statement asserting the "equality of status" of the
provinces, and another declaring that "if any future constitutional
amendment confers powers on one province, these powers must be
available to all provinces." What does this assertion about the equality of provinces mean? Why and how are they equal?

When the Fathers of Confederation debated this subject
between 1864 and 1867, they concluded that, for purposes of allo-
cating seats in the Senate, the new state would encompass three
equal regions—Ontario, Quebec and the Atlantic. When the western provinces joined over the following four decades, it was decided
that they, too, constituted a region and should have twenty-four
Senate seats (six each), as many as each of Ontario, Quebec and the

Maritimes. Newfoundland's six seats were added in 1949. The Yukon and Northwest Territories have been allocated one each.

The notion that each province—not regions—should have the same number of Senate seats, and that this constitutes "equality," is of recent vintage. It probably originates in the construction of the American and Australian senates, in part, but also in the Alberta attitude of belligerence to anything that might suggest it is inferior to another Canadian community. Though it is a Reform Party tenet, as Roger Gibbins and Sonia Arrison note in their book, *Western Visions: Perspectives on the West in Canada*, provincial equality "has never played a prominent role in the regional wings of the Liberal, New Democratic and Progressive Conservative parties."[8] However, it does rise to the surface whenever a public figure suggests that Quebec—a province—should benefit from powers or programs not available to other provinces. The same would be true if Ontario was similarly favoured, but western suspicion has, in recent decades, been directed mainly at Quebec. That the Calgary declaration contains such a principle probably does not mean much, given the declaration's minor place in Canadian public life, but the notion of provincial equality is a troublesome thing that requires definition or abandonment. Again, the parties differ.

II

PROVINCIAL EQUALITY RAISES ANOTHER central issue in western Canadian politics, the status of Quebec and the French language in Canada. Discussion of such matters is, if not unpleasant, at least irritating to most Canadians, including Quebecers. When two seasoned British Columbia commentators, Gordon Wilson, MLA, and Professor John Richards, spoke in Montreal on the topic, they were reviewed scathingly by Ed Bantey, a former Parti Québecois adviser:

> I left with a déjà-vu feeling. If Wilson and Richards are any criterion, English Canada hasn't changed much. It's as patronizing and condescending as ever and, worse, still incapable of coming to grips with Quebec reality. . . . [They] outdid each other vaunting the symbolism of the Calgary Declaration and its offer to recognize Quebec's "unique character," which, presumably, along with poutine, makes it "equal" to Prince Edward Island.[9]

Westerners are often even less flattering about Quebec's sover-eignists. But the bickering does have two sides. Indeed, western parochialism in the face of the metropolitan sophistication exhibited by central Canadians has been a favourite hook among some mem-bers of the "national" media, particularly in Quebec, for decades. Alleged hicks from the West could be relied on to evoke an urbane chuckle whenever the subject was one of the more colourful versions of western conservatism, as represented, say, by the Farmers' March on Ottawa in 1918 or by the Reform Party in the 1990s.

I contend that the political divisions between left and right sketched in the preceding pages are also evident in the West's dis-cussions of Quebec. The fundamental divide is, essentially, compro-mise versus tough love, dialogue versus assertion. And once again, party lines reflect the policy choices.

Are westerners raised in an anti-French, anti-Quebec culture? The blunt answer is yes, unpleasant though it is to contemplate. The explanation lies in one of the fundamental facts of daily life—lan-guage—and in the inevitable patterns of federal institutions.

If you are raised in Europe in a family that assumes you will travel and may work abroad, you have the opportunity to acquire three or four or more languages as a matter of course. Aside from these fortunate people, though, what proportion of the world expects to live and work regularly in several tongues? In western Canada, part of a largely anglophone country in a largely anglo-phone continent, in a world in which English has become the dom-inant language of communication, the possibility of genuine English–French bilingualism is small. It is reserved for a tiny pro-portion of the elites, as the ordinary citizen knows full well. In west-ern Canada, mastery of language other than French, such as Chinese, Cree, German, Ukrainian or Tagalog, is considerably more likely. As former Saskatchewan premier Allan Blakeney told the Task Force on Canadian Unity in 1977:

> Many brave words have been spoken about the
> advantages of living in a country with two cultural
> traditions. Once again, that is a point of view
> which makes sense in Central Canada, but has
> much less meaning for Saskatchewan. The dis-
> tance between Regina and Montreal is greater
> than the distance between Paris and Moscow. Very
> few residents of Saskatchewan have experienced

francophone culture at first hand. The French fact
in Saskatchewan continues to be a matter of bilingual labels and a small community of franco-
phones, smaller by far than the communities of
German or Ukrainian speakers.[10]

The very history of western Canada is a victory of unilingualism
over multilingualism. John Diefenbaker's crusade for "unhyphen-
ated Canadianism" is a direct descendant of the Prairie battles over
languages of instruction in schools in the early twentieth century.

Before francophone Quebecers lament this failure of Canada, it
is well to recall that their ancestors, too, built this country. In the
years of Canada's immigration boom, when the West's decision to
build a unilingual society was taken, Quebecers resisted the fervent
pleas of church, state and family to populate the West. Instead, in
the proportion of eight to one, they followed the shorter trail to
New England, there to abandon the "Frenchness" that those left
behind held so dear.

The language question only became truly urgent—for every
minority language in the world—with the development of a new
phase of communications technology after the Second World War.
Former prime minister Lester Pearson formulated the Canadian
version of this issue in 1963 as one of "bilingualism and biculturalism." He appointed a royal commission whose preliminary report
declared that a crisis in French–English relations, and in the development of the French language, was imminent.

By the time of the commission's final report in 1968–9, however, Pearson's original formulation had been revised. Biculturalism
had been replaced by multiculturalism as one of Canada's fundamental characteristics. Why the change? It reflected the reality of
post–Second World War immigration to Canada's largest cities, but
it owed its political force to western Canada. There, ethnic groups
other than the British and French were assuming the powers of full
Canadian citizenship and defining it in their own terms. As Com-
missioner André Laurendeau discovered in his visits to Prairie cities,
Ukrainians, Germans, Poles and others besieged the public hearings
to insist that the commission recognize a "third force" in Canadian
society. The commission's acquiescence marked a turning point in
Canadian self-perception.

If the one Pearson formulation was rejected outright in western
Canada, the other—official bilingualism in national institutions—

has never found easy acceptance there either. To westerners, it smacks of special favours granted to one group but denied to many others. In competition for federal jobs—the Mounties, the civil service, the prime ministership—it gives an unfair advantage to those who grew up in a French–English environment.

Is the irritation about bilingualism and the insistence on multiculturalism evidence of westerners' prejudice against French-speaking Canadians? No, of course not, if one is speaking about individuals. But yes, if one means that some westerners refuse to make allowances for the Quebec definition of Canadian realities. This hard truth does not mean that compromise is impossible. Rather, it simply points out that deeply held beliefs, the product of hard-won experience, sometimes differ in a large and diverse community. And this is true in the case of biculturalism, a discredited concept in western Canada, and bilingualism, a policy that raises real difficulties for many westerners. When such fundamental national perspectives come into conflict, political institutions become necessary; reason and communication become essential; and compromise, sacrifice or battle constitute three paths forward.

Many Quebec nationalists are repulsed by the patronizing, superior attitude of some who speak English. These Quebecers are justifiably proud of their own history and culture, and determined to remain true to those who sacrificed in the past to maintain the community. Quebec is in most respects a "nation" in the nineteenth-century definition of that term. Only the remarkable history of Canadian politics has ensured that the "right to national self-determination" has not culminated in a sovereign Quebec nation-state.

Quebec is not a province like the others. Neither is it, at this juncture, a stand-alone, just-like-the-others, normal nation. Nor has the Henri Bourassa–Pierre Trudeau vision of a coast-to-coast, two-language Canada, come to pass, though the country is closer to it in the late 1990s than in the late 1950s. Thus, a "Canadian question" remains: How does one accommodate these Quebec aspirations within a federal—but still united—country?

The West's response is, too often, smug. Ed Bantey was right. Westerners are aware that their region has grown slightly more quickly than Quebec. In the 1920s, each held about equal shares of the national population, but since the 1970s, the West's proportion has risen to thirty percent while Quebec's has fallen to twenty-five percent.[11] Westerners are also aware of the relative power of English and French in international conversations. English has become increasingly influential and French has declined in stature. But are western Canadians willing to countenance special measures to ensure the continued vitality of a French-speaking community in Canada? They must come to terms with this challenge.

The country has endured a full generation of constitutional politics in response to this question. Since the early 1960s, in succession, citizens have witnessed Fulton–Favreau, Bi and Bi, the Victoria Declaration, the Parti Québécois victory of 1976, Pépin–Roberts, the 1980 referendum, patriation of the Constitution, Meech Lake, Bélanger–Campeau, Spicer, Beaudoin–Edwards, Charlottetown, the 1995 referendum, the Calgary Framework, the 1998 Supreme Court reference, the Saskatoon (or social union) bargain—and these are just the highlights. Is it any wonder that Quebec is said to be part of the country's fabric? Or that westerners feel their issues have received less attention in the national arena than those of Quebec?

Still, the western Canadian response to the Calgary Framework of 1997, yet another attempt to establish a conversation between Quebec and the other regions, has been very positive. Jeffrey Simpson wrote about a B.C. survey of citizens' responses:

> Nine of 10 British Columbians . . . believe it is important that Quebec remain in Canada. Only about six in 10 accept the "unique character" section [Quebec's National Assembly would have a special role to protect and develop the unique character of Quebec within Canada] of the declaration . . . . Equalization, which takes money out of B.C. for redistribution elsewhere, was supported by 81 percent of respondents . . . . The declaration, in the words of one wise observer, is simply a "candle in the window" for Quebec as it approaches another provincial election and, if the Parti Québécois wins, probably another referendum.[12]

In the West, as in the rest of the country, left and right differ on Quebec issues. Seen from the right, the question is how hard to press the sovereignists. From the left, the question is how to reconcile two very different perceptions of the modern world's cultural dynamics. The left speaks softly, anxious to understand and to find accommodations. The right speaks with greater assertiveness, convinced that, by conveying forcefully its sense of cold realities, it will sway the uncommitted Québécois or, alternatively, provide an advantageous position in the negotiations that follow a yes vote.

Right and left are tough or soft on all the issues of the post-1995 discussions. Should the legal status of secession be referred to the Supreme Court? Should other Canadians be permitted to participate in the drafting of a "clear" question on the referendum ballot? Should other Canadians be permitted to participate in the establishment of a "clear majority" threshold in a referendum? Should portions of Quebec be permitted to secede from a new nation after a yes vote? Should other Canadians now prepare a list of items to be negotiated in the event of a yes vote? Should other Canadians now establish a process to be followed in the negotiations? To each question, those on the left take the soft option while those on the right take the hard.

Right and left also differ on how to address Quebec's concerns in the days leading up to a referendum. The key subject is decentralization. The right favours stronger provinces, wishes to weaken the national government and campaigns fiercely on the need to reduce duplication of effort by the two levels of government. It is noteworthy that the first draft of the Calgary Declaration was prepared by the Business Council on National Issues, a lobby group supported by Canada's largest corporations.

The left supports a strong central government that is able to consider new areas of social legislation and can deliver the wealth redistribution implicit in the present system of equalization payments. In the Manitoba and Saskatchewan hearings, the left also emphasized the need to recognize aboriginal aspirations more fully in the Calgary Declaration.[13] Indeed, the New Democrats in Manitoba placed two of their aboriginal MLAs on the committee drafting the provincial response to emphasize this concern.

It may not seem like a typical left–right debate, but western discussions about the place of the French language in Canadian public life and the place of Quebec in Confederation do conform to the same patterns as debates about taxation and spending policies.

III

FEDERALISM AS A FORM OF government is more complicated than legislative union. Could the inevitable struggle between central and provincial governments become so predictable, so boring or even so irritating, that citizens turn away from political conversation entirely?

We live in an age when public conversation relies on the short snatches of detail built up by television news, radio headlines and tabloid newspapers. Such venues are ideally suited to the telling of a personal story. Yet, as in any age, a public issue demands more sustained analysis than most of us can muster most of the time. If, for their economic survival, our news outlets depend exclusively on sales in an open market, it is easy to predict which part of our natures they will appeal to. Thus, those who conduct one side of our community conversation—the journalists—will permit such stories as OJ, Diana and Monica to overshadow the information that the other side—the public—needs if it is to shape community policy.

This is the problem of Canadian federalism. In a series of rulings starting with the patriation of the Constitution in 1981–2, the Supreme Court has reinforced the essential place of provinces (not the equality of provinces, but the *role* of provinces), in the Canadian political system. Thus, in its August 1998 ruling on whether Quebec had a right to unilateral secession in Canadian or international law, the court said no, and then added the absolutely pivotal qualification that "a clear majority vote in Quebec on a clear question in favour of secession would confer democratic legitimacy on the secession initiative which all of the other participants in Confederation would have to recognize." A province, in short, has the right to secede. A *Globe and Mail* editorial observed with admirable calm:

> In constitutional law, Canada is now one and divisible, perhaps the only country on Earth to make it official.... In practice, the court has amended the Canadian Constitution to include a basic secession clause—the most aggressive act of judicial "reading in" in Canadian history.[14]

The Supreme Court ruling invokes a number of fundamental principles, no one of which transcends the others, including constitutionalism and the rule of law, respect for the rights of individuals and minorities (including therein aboriginal people), the operation of democracy and, of central purpose in the present discussion, "the principle of federalism." The court suggests that Canadians adopted the political form of the federal state in 1867 "to reconcile diversity with unity." Thus, "the social and demographic reality of Quebec explains the existence of the province of Quebec as a political unit and, indeed, was one of the essential reasons for establishing a federal structure for the Canadian union in 1867."

Canada embraces not just one province but ten, as well as three territories and a federal government. Given open debate and choices arrived at democratically, the Supreme Court judge declared, the provinces and the federal government—together—must be able to reconcile diversity with unity. A *Vancouver Sun* editorial on the judgment summarized: "The federal and provincial governments share political power, which is allocated by the Constitution. So federalism and the Constitution express the political interconnectedness, while our democratic system commits us to 'acknowledge and address' dissenting voices."[15]

There is an admirable balance in the Supreme Court judgment. Its decision to set out fundamental principles of the nation but not to place a priority on any one—equality or diversity, majority rule or minority dissent—represents two wise choices. The third pillar of their ruling is reliance on the political sphere as the arena of debate and the means of resolving disputes. In a period of low public regard for politics, the reminder that the political system plays a pivotal role in the community is salutary.

Such a reminder returns us to western Canadian debates about federalism. Western Conservatives and members of the Reform Party are, in general, decentralizers; western New Democrats and federal Liberals are, in general, supporters of a strong central government. Reformers actually see power differently from socialists. According to Tom Flanagan, Preston Manning views power as autonomy, not as the ability to control or assist others. Thus, if the sphere of personal or family authority can be expanded, if referenda can provide effective means of consulting the people about their wishes, or if economic freedom can be increased and government redistribution of wealth reduced, then these are means of facilitating the exercise of power—an individual's sphere of freedom—in a community. A Liberal or New Democrat would say, in contrast, that they are steps towards the relinquishment of power.[16]

This chapter has sketched the political circumstance of western Canada in broad strokes. And indeed, exceptions to its generalizations about left and right, centralizers versus decentralizers, are easily found. This is especially true if one looks for conflicts between provincial and federal wings of the same party. Indeed, provincial wings always believe that provinces need more power, deserve more tax room and see the local circumstance more clearly; but move under the federal umbrella and, presto, Ottawa has a broader, more nuanced perception of the big picture and must, of necessity, accept the obligation to promote common standards across the land. Voilà, you might say—we have established the usual ground rules of a federal system. Or, if you are inclined to be less positive, you have discovered the conditions for more federal–provincial bickering and for citizen turn-off and tune-out. Such debates simply go with the territory in a federal system.[17]

My point, however, is slightly different. I am arguing that individuals inevitably come down on various sides of the vast numbers of questions that arise in public discussions. It happens as often as not that their positions are contradictory, if measured by the abstract principles of markets and civil liberties. Parties, by contrast, make a fetish of consistency. In particular, liberty and equality, majority rule and minority dissent, and power as individual autonomy or as collective control constitute litmus tests of left and right in western Canada as everywhere else. On federalism, on family and civil relations, on "free" markets versus government intervention, on ethnic and aboriginal and affirmative action issues, there is a left and a right in western Canada.

REFERENCES

1. Stephen Harper's view that Canadians lament their "lack of real representation" is cited in Gordon Gibson, "Lessons from the hepatitis C battle" *Globe and Mail* 5 May 1998, A23.

2. Edward Greenspan, "Manning pushes 'united alternative'" *Globe and Mail* 1 June 1998, A4.

3. Judy Rebick, "Women find a place in Reform—at home" *Ottawa Citizen* 2 June 1998, A17.

4. Tom Flanagan, "Reform needs coherent [social] policy" *Winnipeg Free Press* 7 March 1998, A15; editorial "Reform throws party at court's expense" *Globe and Mail* 11 June 1998, A22; Frances Russell, "Reform sidles toward the centre" *Winnipeg Free Press* 4 March 1998, A10.

5. Preston Manning, "The Case for Reform of the Senate" delivered in the House of Commons 20 April 1998 (typescript).

6. Abolitionists include Gordon Gibson, "A blueprint for disbanding the Senate" *Globe and Mail* 23 June 1998, A23; Robert Bragg, "Abolish the Senate" *Calgary Herald* 14 June 1998, A15. Supporters of an initial election of "Senators-in-waiting" include David Bercuson and Barry Cooper, "The logic behind an elected Senate" and Tom Flanagan, "One day, we may elect our senators" *Globe and Mail*, 8 August (D2) and 13 August (A19) 1998, respectively.

7. I would like to thank Casey Vander Ploeg and Robert Roach, research analysts at the Canada West Foundation, for their willingness to share their enthusiasm for the foundation and for political ideas. The foundation's 120–odd publications since 1980 are listed in its *Annual Report 1997*. The Senate reform proposal was published as *Electing Alberta's Senators* (Canada West Foundation, March 1998). The Foundation now publishes a quarterly newsletter "The Foundation Files" 1, 1 (June 1998).

8. Roger Gibbins and Sonia Arrison, *Western Visions: Perspectives on the West in Canada* (Peterborough: Broadview Press 1995) p. 58.

The British Columbia Liberals have adopted a decentralist stance in recent years and, thus, constitute an exception to this general rule.

9. Ed Bantey, "Strange view from ROC" Montreal *Gazette* 8 February 1998.

10. cited in Gibbins and Arrison, *Western Vision*s p. 119.

11. There is nothing sacred about population projections. Architect Arthur Erickson predicts a population of 10 to 25 million for a Vancouver super-city, ca. 2040, but provincial demographers project a slowdown in the rate of growth—perhaps 6 million in all of B.C. by 2030; Ken MacQueen, "B.C.'s population growth to slow" *Vancouver Sun* 22 August 1998, A1, 15.
Who knows what lies in store for Alberta? For the French language, worldwide and in Quebec? The combination of factors is too great to be sure that the slight shift of population towards the West and away from Quebec will continue.

12. Jeffrey Simpson, "B.C.'s eye-popping levels of support for the Calgary declaration" *Globe and Mail* 13 February 1998.

13. *Report of the Manitoba Legislative Task Force on Canadian Unity* (typescript 1998); Canada West Foundation *Final Conference Report: Saskatchewan: Finding Common Ground on Canada's Future* (Calgary: 1997).

14. Editorial "Confederation is voluntary" *Globe and Mail* 21 August 1998.

15. Editorial "Provinces counted in by Quebec ruling: The Supreme Court's decision contains a reminder of why federalism was chosen as the political framework for a fledgling nation, and how that framework continues to serve the country's best interests" *Vancouver Sun* 22 August 1998, A22.

16. Tom Flanagan, *Waiting for the Wave: The Reform Party and Preston Manning* (Toronto: Stoddart 1995) pp. 28–32.

17. The "Saskatoon agreement" on rules to guide the two levels of government on matters arising within "Canada's social union," reached in August 1998, is simply one illustration of the eternal federal–provincial balancing act. A revised version was approved by Ottawa and nine provinces (but not Quebec) in February 1999.

Conclusion

The differences between West and East today are not so profound that they challenge Canada's national existence. There are disagreements, of course, as the results of the federal elections during the 1990s demonstrate clearly. Moreover, there is a sense in public and media discussions that the regions are drifting ever farther apart. But, as the preceding pages suggest, I question whether these divisions are out of the ordinary.

My belief is that, as happens from time to time in the history of a large and diverse country, Canadians' understanding of one another is becoming out-of-date. The country is changing rapidly, right along with the rest of the world. In this increasingly global age, the inherited explanations of each region are lapsing into meaninglessness. They must be refurbished or replaced.

The ten-gallon hats that represent one image of the West speak of the freedom of the frontier and a chance to begin life again, whether on ranch or farm, in the new West. Today, there are many fewer cowboys or farmers. Indeed, what is striking about the West today is the pressure on farm families to make ends meet and the extraordinary productivity of the few who remain compared to their counterparts of a half-century ago. A man who moved from Edmonton to Winnipeg described his trip through rural Saskatchewan on a beautiful Sunday morning in August 1998 and how his car slipped down silent highways, not another vehicle or person in sight, for the entire morning. I felt the same sensation of barrenness when I took my mother to her home village near Saskatoon. It was once a thriving community that knit together dozens of family sagas from

Ontario, Quebec and the Maritimes, Britain and Ukraine, Sweden
and the United States. When I was a child, it had seemed to embrace
four or five geographically distinct subdistricts, each with its own
sports day and picnic. But as we descended from the hills north of
town and gazed across a now-treeless plain that swept thirty kilo-
metres away to the Allan Hills, all the old schools and sports
grounds had disappeared, most of the farmhouses and shelter belts
had vanished, and even the village itself was a scattered, forlorn rem-
nant of another era.

Get over it, you might reply and, indeed, this is good advice. But
one can still pause to commemorate or lament the passing of good
societies, the eclipse of the works of generations of community-
builders. Like the aboriginal people who had travelled these plains
before them, the pioneer settlers have faded from the scene. The
eagle feathers in an encampment, the cowboy hat on an old farmer,
the jellied salads at a fall supper all evoke images of another time.

A different West had taken its place. It is built on a revised
economy and changed political concerns. This book has tried to
outline both, and in the process rescue the time-honoured symbols
and provide them with renewed meaning.

As for the eagle-feather image, if it has not struck you recently,
consider instead the scarlet coats of the Nisga'a women who entered
the British Columbia Legislature at the start of the 1998 treaty
debate. Or the photographs of Elijah Harper, lone aboriginal member of the Manitoba legislature in 1990, casting the one vote that
destroyed the Meech Lake constitutional accord. That vote was cast
on behalf of all Native Canadians. It was a protest against the omis-
sion of their concerns from the round of constitutional amendments. Throughout the session, Harper carried an eagle feather in
his hand.

The feather can stand for a wider range of community
expressions, too. At a Caribbean community gathering in Winnipeg in November 1998, Glen Murray, the gay man who had
been elected mayor just days before, brought greetings on behalf
of the city to a group that was overwhelmingly immigrant
and black. His emphatic declaration, "I am speaking from one
minority to another," was greeted with a roar of approval. It was a
statement about the changing composition of the population in
western Canada's larger cities. And if one component in these
new communities is from Asia and others are from the Caribbean,
Latin America and Africa, then yet another comes from rural and

northern communities across the West and is aboriginal in heritage. The eagle feather, like the rainbow, represents these new forces in western Canadian society.

The ten-gallon hat still represents the freedom of the frontier. Now, however, freedom is defined by its bearers as absence of government, reduced taxes, fewer regulations and survival of the fittest on the open (both continental and global) range. If it takes corporation-sponsored publicity agencies, student conferences and political campaigns to maintain such freedoms, then that's the price that supporters of a right-wing perspective will happily pay.

The brightly-coloured salads may represent the left. They are not unique to the West but, as the singer Connie Kaldor reminds us, they did travel from thousands of western kitchens to decorate the tables of thousands of community fundraising dinners undertaken by church, school and political party. If the ten-gallon hat speaks of competition and the individual, this humble near-vegetable speaks of co-operation, community and equality. It will never occupy the centre of a national flag, but the jellied salad in church basement and community hall also contributed to the national medicare plan.

One might question why the West should be seen as a single unit. The main reasons, I think, are the size of the country, the history and the composition of its various communities, and the governmental system chosen by the fathers of Confederation.

The national image of a single West has greater claim to existence today than at any time in Canadian history. This is partly due to the relative economic decline of Manitoba and Saskatchewan, and the relative rise of Alberta and British Columbia. But it has developed, too, because the distinctive pattern of income fluctuations, the emergence of a knowledge and service economy, and the presence in each province of comparable resource industries and comparable aboriginal and immigrant communities have caused the eclipse of the Prairies and the Coast. The West is an increasingly relevant regional generalization.

The notion of a West is also sustained by politics. One might think that this was merely the creation of the national political media. But the Reform Party and neoconservative views are real enough and do have a base in Alberta and British Columbia. As long as Reform in particular and conservatism in general hold a preponderance of western seats in the House of Commons, their supporters will attempt to appropriate the West and to claim that they represent a monolithic conservative community. Political fortunes change, though, so don't be misled by a particular historical moment.

The idea of the West is also due to the existence of four provincial political systems, each distinct, each travelling to its own rhythm, each subject to accidents of its own personalities and parties. Like the four governments of Atlantic Canada, the stories of four western provincial systems are, for those outside the territory, too much to bother with. Enough, say the outsiders. Give me the short version—cowboy hats or jellied salads?

The reply is more complicated. There is no single "western" view on any of the issues that confront the nation. There are four provinces in western Canada and at least two sides in each political debate. And all have ambitions to lead the nation, or at least persuade it to see the world from their points of view.

We all have to refurbish our pictures of the vast regions of the Canadian archipelago if we are to understand how they relate to one another and to our own experience. The inherited image of a downtrodden West always being discriminated against by central Canada, is less relevant today, though it would only take a moment and another political decision like the CF-18 contract to revive it. In its place is a region influenced by the same globalizing forces that are reshaping everyone. Cole Harris's observation, noted in the Introduction, that the West is affected less by family genealogy and more by movement, technology, markets, and memories of other places is true. The societies and people of western Canada are undergoing rapid and profound change. The West's image in the minds of Canadians may owe much to history, but the region in which westerners live owes more to economic and political change. The time-honoured images of the West, whether ten-gallon hats, eagle feathers or jellied salads, may still be relevant, but only if they are reinterpreted in light of today's realities.

Index

Pearson, Lester, 174

Population, 30, 50–1, 56, 59–61, 68, 85, 100, 113–4, 136, 175, 182

Prince Albert, 101, 108–9

Racism, 57–62, 108–9, 136–45, 147

Reform Party, *xvii*, 44, 78, 95, 139, 144–5, 151–3, 159, 168–81, 185

Regina, 100, 108, 113

Region, *xv–xvii*, 4–12, 14–23, 35–6, 40, 47, 50–1, 55–7, 60, 62, 145, 155, 171–7, 179–80, 183–6

Resource industries (oil, gas, forest, farm, potash) (see water), 26–39, 47, 70–2, 86–9, 103–4

Riel, Louis, 4, 53, 144

Roman Catholic church, 58, 151

Romanow, Roy, 105, 107, 110, 113, 162

Royal Commission on Aboriginal People, 143

Royal Commission on Bilingualism and Biculturalism, 61–2

Royal Commission on the Economic Union, 28

Rural society and economy, 26–39, 112, 117–20, 152, 154–5

Saskatchewan, 6, 11, 41, 58–9, 99–113, 114, 116, 120–1, 126, 152, 154–5, 162–5, 173, 185

Saskatoon, 100, 176, 183

Scriver, Stephen, 126–7

Senate of Canada (and Triple E), 169–72, 181

Service and knowledge industries, 35, 42–9, 96, 103

Sexuality, 148–55

Smith, Melvin, 77–8

Social democracy, 21–2, 70, 87–8, 105, 158–67

Social gospel, 22

Social union, 176, 182

Supreme Court of Canada, 54–5, 73–9, 109–10, 152–3, 156–7, 169, 177

Transportation, 104–5

Treaties (Aboriginal-Canada), 53, 72–9

Unions, 70–3

United States of America, 16, 18, 28–9, 32–9, 53, 58–9, 62, 79, 90, 93–4, 104, 114, 125, 127, 141, 161, 163, 169, 174

Urban society and urban places (see cities by name), 30, 37, 46, 51, 67–70, 79–81, 84–6, 100, 112, 152

Vancouver, 8–9, 45, 49, 67, 69, 79–81, 85, 114, 117, 123, 126, 135–8, 151, 159

Victoria, 67, 69

Water, 27, 35, 99, 116

Wheat economy, 15–17, 19–23, 27–32

Winnipeg, 5, 114–7, 124–8, 136, 150, 162, 184